Poppies
Pomp &
People

I dedicate this book to Oskar, Lola, Natasha, Florence and Hector. You and all the other young people will help to shape the future. For today, The Tower of London offers fine examples of honouring and recording history, of preserving parts of our heritage, of aspiring for excellence in standards, not least towards all visitors. This should be preserved well into the future.

Poppies Pomp & People

A year in the life of the Tower of London

CHRISTOPHER WEST

The Choir Press

First published in the United Kingdom in 2016 by
The Choir Press

ISBN 978-1-910864-75-3

Contents

Yeoman Warder in ceremonial dress

Acknowledgements

Lord Dannatt, the Governor for permission and Deputy Governor for sound advice and liaison, the Canon Chaplain, head of Press Department and Pauline Stobbs, numerous members of staff at the Tower, particularly Yeoman Gaoler, Huw Lloyd and other members of the congregation,

Most particular thanks to Michelle Sanderson for her extensive 'book support skills, patience and advice,' Jia Chuan, Penelope Shipley, Jason Akande, Josh Rees, Sarah Wesson, Michelle Seidel, Gwen Hewett and Camilla. John Raphael, Riz Marcello, my fine new computer (though strictly not the software). Publisher Miles Bailey, Rachel Woodman and Adrian Sysum have been outstanding with helping me at Choir Press.

The West Gate, which is currently the main entrance.

Preface

Why the book? Fortunately, I live near the Tower of London and visit most Sundays for the morning chapel service. I quickly learned that even friends close by knew very little about what goes on and how it works. Yes, we admire the Tower and know a bit about its history, the Beefeaters and the Crown Jewels. But do most of us know that many families and other people live there? That the Yeoman Warders are not only senior and successful armed forces veterans, but high-flying experts in subjects ranging from hotel management to lifeboat drill? The chapel choir is one of the finest of its type in the country; how? The Tower doesn't cost the taxpayer a penny; why not? The place is teeming with personnel whose overriding goals are striving for excellence in providing the best experience for the millions of visitors per annum and preserving this national treasure for the future. How do they achieve it?

From the beginning, I felt a growing depth of respect and awe (I guess like most visitors), and I quickly learned that the Yeoman Warders are experts in storytelling – highly articulate, able to hold attention and extremely humorous, so they are excellent performers. But further observation leads to a far deeper understanding of these people's gifts – constantly vigilant and communicating as a team, tirelessly smiling for the camera and giving answers to an endless array of questions. The support staff are equally essential to this success: the management and the dedicated more junior staff that make up this unique group.

This book is intended as a light read, so it is brief; sadly, this means that only some people can be featured or mentioned, despite their importance, likeability or whatever. There are gardeners, key administrators, Jewel House and White Tower staff and so many more. Thank you, all of you, who help to make the place succeed and have helped me with information.

So many strong personalities live and work together in this small, walled, world-famous fortress. Its community is unique, to be admired and cherished proudly, both by our nation and by our visitors.

Replica in the Wakefield Tower of the throne used by King Edward I

Foreword

Having stood proudly on the north bank of the River Thames for nearly a thousand years, the White Tower at the heart of the Tower of London has been witness to the full spectrum of colour, drama, excitement and despair, but never before had it seen its moat filled to overflowing with a sea of red poppies. 2014 was that year, as the Nation began its centenary commemorations of the First World War. Tower enthusiast Chris West was present throughout that year and has recorded the events of that extraordinary period in this enchanting book. He has produced a one-man 'fly on the wall' documentary account of life in the Tower of London when Blood Swept Lands and Seas of Red captured the Nation's imagination, and heart.

In a very unobtrusive way, Chris West made sure that he was present at every event – large and small – during 2014 and 2015. He watched, listened and recorded all that was going on during those years. He has captured the thoughts of a very large number of those involved in the life of the Tower from the Yeoman Warders to the Chaplain, to the Constable, to the curators, and not forgetting the families of Tower residents nor the visitors who flood through the gates every day. Over the years, many histories have been written about the Tower and the great events that have occurred within its walls, but this is a record of life today, proving that the Tower of London is living history and not just a relic of the past.

The centrepiece for Chris West's book is the installation of 888,246 ceramic poppies – one for every British and Colonial soldier who lost their life in the First World War. Each poppy represented a life lost and a family shattered, and it was this personal and individual representation of sacrifice that made this commemorative event so special. Chris West records the army of volunteers from around the country and around the world who planted the poppies from July 2014 onwards, and then returned in November to pick them, as the poppies began their individual journeys to the homes of those who had bought them. Those who died at Ypres, on the Somme or in Gallipoli never went home, but these poppies, in their memory, are now cherished throughout our land, and abroad. And the sale of the poppies generated almost £10 million to help improve the lives of our wounded, injured and sick soldiers from today's wars. The Tower of London was very proud to play host to this great endeavour, and Chris West has captured the story in a delightful way. I congratulate him for his achievement and commend this book to all who want to get a real feel for life inside the Tower of London today.

Richard Dannatt

General the Lord Dannatt GCB CBE MC DL
Constable, HM Tower of London 2009–2016

Part One
A year at the Tower

Yeoman Gaoler with his axe

January 2015

January 31st 1606: Guy Fawkes and three others were dragged from the Tower and executed at Westminster.

January 2nd: The Tower Welcomes Its First 2015 Visitors

This dedicated community, bracing itself in readiness, is appreciative, proud and well aware of the privilege of living here, an award often regarded as the pinnacle of an already distinguished and successful career. But the holiday is over, and for the Yeoman Warders (known around the world as Beefeaters) this is no sinecure, as maybe in years gone by, or straightforward reward for previous success; it's now back to sustained, skilled hard work. There are two imperatives to maintain: continuing the striving for excellence by giving every visitor the best experience possible, while preserving our priceless national asset for future generations.

> *There is a sort of balance between guardianship and delighting the customers. So giving everybody a fantastic time while preserving the integrity and fabric of our buildings, which is sometimes a really delicate balancing act … We have amazing collections and excellent partners on site with the Royal Armoury and the Royal Collection Trust with the Crown Jewels. So there is all that and everyone wants to make this a fantastic experience. We do aim to give everyone a sense of the history.*
>
> Megan Gooch, Learning Producer

Chief Yeoman Warder

> *There's a lot of work going on just to make this even better for the visitor – because we are such an infamous, famous site that there are so many stories to tell, and you've got to try and work out, from 900 years of history, where do you even pick them out?*
>
> Cate Milton, Ops Programme Coordinator

Welcome at the entrance

The Tower of London is one of the most visited tourist attractions in the United Kingdom. People enter through the West Gate and staff do all they can to keep queues moving efficiently and quickly. The Yeoman Warders are constantly alert to detail and supervision, while also being entertaining, helpful, and welcoming.

Junior school group

One of the main attractions is the Jewel House; owing to clever design and a moving escalator, many people can pass through per hour, and they can go around as many times as they want. Visitors who don't want to use the headphone guides (now in a number of languages) soon come to the gathering area for the next tour, given by one of the world-famous Yeoman Warders.

A class from a local primary school are the first to arrive. Up to a thousand children are facilitated in groups each day, and they are highly valued by the Tower. Katie Newton and her colleagues are ready and waiting. Her title is Site Facilitator, Operations Team, Learning & Engagement, Historic Royal Palaces (referred to as HRP, the charitable organisation responsible for the Tower; more at http://www.hrp.org.uk).

The work of this department goes so much deeper than just communicating with schools and providing on-site facilities; it is finely tuned to its unique opportunity to support and grow people's understanding, young and old, of the stories that make up the history of these royal establishments.

January 4th: Epiphany Service at the Chapel Royal, St Peter ad Vincula

The Constable greeting the Lord Mayor and the Lady Mayoress

This first Sunday gives the events calendar an excellent start. The Lord Mayor of the City of London is one of today's main guests; he and the Lady Mayoress are seen here being greeted by the Constable, Lord Dannatt. This annual occasion supports the work of the charity Livability and its Chief Executive, Dave Webber, is the other main guest. Regular members of the congregation and visitors are joined by staff and supporters of Livability, a Christian charity which engages 'disability and community'.

The Lord Mayor is wearing the historically significant Collar of Esses, the chain of office once used by Sir Thomas More as Chancellor of England; his shrine lies in the chapel crypt. Special permission to wear this item is granted on few occasions, this being one because St Peter ad Vincula has royal status. Similarly, Canon Roger Hall MBE, the Tower's Chaplain (seen here escorting the Lord Mayor), wears scarlet to signify the status of the Chapel Royal.

The Chaplain joins the group

As always, the congregation is gently but firmly marshalled by the duty Yeoman Warder – not straightforward because this annual service is well supported by Livability members, so many of the seats need to be reserved, on top of seating the regulars and other visitors within a short space of time. The professional choir members have little time to rehearse, so they need to be uninterrupted until fifteen minutes before the services start.

Canon Roger is close at hand and very welcoming to regulars and visitors.

During the service, the Chief Executive quietly, yet with great compassion, addressed the continuing work of the charity, deeply appreciative of the support given by the Lord Mayor and the Chapel (this is the charity's nineteenth year at the Tower). Following the service, Lord Mayor Yarrow visited the crypt to pay tribute to Sir Thomas More, then joined the congregation for refreshments.

The Lord Mayor commented:

> I was delighted to see the Chapel Royal of St Peter ad Vincula up close and to explore the burial place of Sir Thomas More, who gave his name to the Lord Mayor's magnificent chain of office. The significance is even more pronounced this year, with the TV adaptation of Hilary Mantel's Wolf Hall bringing a new audience to the story of Sir Thomas, Thomas Cromwell, Anne Boleyn and others buried here. It is a reminder of the history on which is built London's successes in business, politics and culture.
>
> Alderman Alan Yarrow, Lord Mayor of the City of London

Dave Webber also commented:

> The heritage and history of St Peter ad Vincula, the exceptional music, choir and the uplifting spirit of the congregation is very special for us. This event provides a valuable higher profile and [the opportunity] to engage with a wide group of people for prayer and sharing our charity's message. As a charity founded firmly on Christian ethos and principles, we are immensely grateful to the Governor and Chaplain for the privilege to be part of the life of the chapel and this very special place.

All are invited to the regular services at the Tower. Canon Roger is most welcoming and the congregation is growing with many regular local users and visitors. Just arrive at the Main Gate in good time and mention to the Yeoman Warder that you are here for the service – there is no entry fee or need to queue. As well as Chaplain of the Tower, Canon Roger is also one of the Queen's Chaplains and Chaplain to today's guest, the Lord Mayor of the City of London.

Service details are at: http://www.hrp.org.uk/tower-of-london/history-and-stories/the-chapel-of-st-peter-ad-vincula/news-events-and-services/

Canon Roger Hall

January 7th: Upcoming Major Exhibition

Chris Gidlow, Live Interpretation Manager at Historic Royal Palaces, has an important meeting today. He is planning ideas for a major exhibition to mark the 600th anniversary of the Battle of Agincourt, which will run from October to January. These events bring new life to the Tower, inviting people to return time after time, instead of the old style, visiting once as a child and then perhaps once or twice as an adult. In addition to the exhibitions, he also directs the professional actors and arranges their themes and stories. He is planning to run a new event, which he describes as:

Performing 'Beat the Block'

> *'Beat the Block', a participation event for families visiting at the February half-term, about Henry VIII's female prisoners. We decided not to have Anne Boleyn and Catherine Howard, who are already quite well-covered, so decided to focus on famous people of whom you didn't know what actually happened to them. So each of the women would be presenting their case and the Headsman would then ask visitors whether they would prefer them to be executed or pardoned – it's their choice and in their hands. It's really quite shocking when you get to the end. There was Alice Wolf, the pirate, and Elizabeth Barton, the Holy Maid of Kent; they got the thumbs down. Apart from the King's niece, who got off, everybody else got executed! It was very poignant.*

Actors engaging the public

I have now watched a number of the actors' performances and it is clever, the way that they can attract considerably sized audiences without getting in the way of the main traffic flow, which gets very heavy at busy times. The acting is to a high standard and carefully thought through. Their costumes are impressive and they hold the audiences for quite long periods. Comments are enthusiastic and the children get deeply involved and excited. Chris Gidlow combines extensive theatrical and production talent with a shrewd business sense, dedicated to bringing in more people to visit the Tower.

January 10th: Interview with John Scott, External Security Manager

John's non-military background makes him unusual, his previous career having been in design and advertising. Soon after joining the Tower, he was asked to take over external security management and was hence 'taught to shout', parade-ground fashion. He quickly adapted from reserved, reflective and advisory to pushier and outgoing. Previous skills have been useful in producing training programmes in security and customer care for the Tower.

Day to day, John leads the team that ensures that visitors enter correctly with passes or the appropriate tickets. On busy days, this can be extremely demanding because the queues need to be dealt with efficiently, with as few hiccups as possible, often in poor weather conditions. He is often to be seen 'leading from the front', collecting tickets and walking at speed from area to area (dressing in a broad range of smart suits and snazzy waistcoats).

John Scott

Hillsborough Castle is now administered by HRP and John was sent there to give a talk about customer care. He was recently nominated by colleagues to attend a Buckingham Palace garden party.

John played an unusual role on the same day as the Queen's recent visit. Prince Michael was on a separate visit, invited by the Constable. He was delayed on leaving the Queen's House, prior to being driven to the moat entrance. On learning that no one was available to open the Prince's car door, John (now past his youthful best) had to run fast from Queen's House to near the main gate, down to Water Lane along the cobbles. Somewhat flushed and short of breath, he steadied himself by putting one hand on the door, before opening it for the Prince to alight … then, looking down, he noticed a huge hand mark left on the highly polished surface. To his great relief, the chauffeur quickly produced spray polish (labelled 'by Royal appointment') to resolve the issue quietly and with great dignity.

John is retiring after twenty years at the Tower and is now training for a further career in sports massage therapy.

January 14th: Work Commences on Dismantling the White Tower Steps

A temporary structure is ready to be put in place. See October 22nd for the full story.

January 21st: Sir Winston Churchill's Memorial Wreath

This wreath of laurel leaves, surmounted by the iconic 'V' for Victory symbol in gold, has been specially designed and made by the Royal Poppy Factory and is to be laid on the water of the River Thames, opposite the Houses of Parliament, to commemorate the culmination of Winston Churchill's state funeral on 30th January 1965. It will lie close to the altar until collection on the 30th.

Churchill's memorial wreath

January 26th: Music Director's 'Twenty Years at The Tower' Celebration Concert at St Peter's

Colm Carey

Colm Carey is Master of Music, Chapels Royal, HM Tower of London, and he celebrated his twenty years at the Tower by performing in a concert with friends. Drinks were served at the end and I chatted with a trumpeter who had just played in a stunning duet with Colm; we agreed that the concert was excellent and I mentioned having difficulty writing about how Colm had achieved such high standards at the Tower. He cheerfully said he would send me an email on the subject and I thanked him. I realised that he was a friend of Colm's and a gifted musician, but imagine my thrill when I received his email (set out below). I had no idea that he was also the Principal of the Royal Academy of Music – it's hard to imagine a more qualified tribute or better explanation.

Creating a durable corpus of friends, supporters and professional musicians requires a special kind of flair and Colm has established just that at the Tower. This was wonderfully evident in Colm's recent 'concert-party.' He and I started playing trumpet and organ concerts together just after he finished his postgraduate studies in Geneva, and we even made a couple of half-decent CDs, but over the years, we've pursued different paths. So, to play a part in that event rekindled many happy memories. But most of all it reminded me of all the musical and personal qualities which make Colm a 'one-off' as an organist: a top-drawer virtuosic capability but also someone who wants to communicate and share his love of music as widely as possible. Leaving little to chance, he supports his musical colleagues with his life. When we played, he opened the copy of the work we performed last in about 2000 (Fritz Werner's little sonata, simply called 'Duo') and off we went for our rehearsal. It was wonderful just 'clicking in' immediately after all those years. He told me – rightly – not to rush in all the places I always used to rush! (My copy even says, 'Don't Rush'!) Same Colm. Same antennae. It was marvellous listening to his unmistakeable playing, always so warmly settled, controlled and serious but never dull. He draws the listener in with sound and makes us forget he's playing an instrument often laden with limited associations. The 'anniversary' revealed how an excellent musician can draw a community together towards understanding the resonating purpose and potential of high-level music-making in as special and unique an environment as St Peter's at the Tower.

Prof. Jonathan Freeman-Attwood, Principal,
Royal Academy of Music

Colm is considered equally successful directing the choir, which is acknowledged as one of the finest of its type in the UK. Colm discusses this on June 26th.

With Colm Carey's firm direction, our music excels weekly. Today, an extra dimension was provided by choir member Jamie Hall, who also sings bass baritone with the BBC Singers and has written a piece that was commissioned by Colm for the choir, which was performed today. Its title is 'The Lord Has Arisen'.

Jamie said:

Colm again

It was a pleasure to write and that it happened at all is reflective of Chaplain Roger and Colm's wish to support the choir both inside and outside their role in the life of the chapel; that's quite unusual on the London church circuit.

January 30th: Sir Winston Churchill; Fiftieth Anniversary of his Funeral Commemorated

Today's commemoration began with Yeoman Serjeant Peter McGowran and colleagues, who marched the wreath from St Peter ad Vincula diagonally across the Tower. They handed it over to the

Marching out the Churchill Wreath

Escort ready to take the wreath to the Havengore

Havengore *retracing Churchill's burial route*

military escort, which carried it in procession, led by a Scots pipe band, through St Katharine Docks to the *Havengore*, retracing the voyage when the same vessel carried Churchill's coffin upriver to Westminster as part of his state funeral fifty years ago. On board was Canon Roger Hall, Chaplain of the Tower of London, who led prayers before the wreath was cast into the water in front of the Houses of Parliament. The pictures on page 9 show the Yeoman Warders marching out with the Churchill memorial wreath, handover to escort in procession, and (*above*) *Havengore*. Tower Bridge saluted the occasion by rising to 90 degrees instead of the customary 45 degrees.

Constable of Her Majesty's Royal Palace and Fortress of the Tower
Lord Dannatt begins his last full year as Constable, expecting to retire in July 2016. Change and development seem to arrive faster than ever before (think of technology or the buildings within a mile of the Tower) and today's Constable has risen to the challenge.

The Constable

He has brought in his vibrant personality and authority; much more than just a figurehead, he is deeply involved and committed to the life of the Tower. Former army chief Lord Dannatt is the 159th Constable and, being the sovereign's representative in the Tower, he enjoys the privilege of direct access to the Queen, as head of state. The role was created by William the Conqueror and has continued for nearly a thousand years.

Leaving his residence

The Constable lodges in Queen's House, which was built around 1540, reputed to be the oldest timber-framed structure in London, having survived the Great Fire of London in 1666. The public rooms are tastefully adorned with an excellent collection of historical artefacts and furniture, and the views from the windows are onto the Thames. The decision was made in 2011 that the

Inspection for the State Parade

Constable should lodge in the house, previously the Resident Governor's quarters, when he is in London, but that others should have some access to the history within the house. Since then, Lord Dannatt and his wife have opened up their residence extensively, hosting and welcoming scores of people and working with devotion to raising money on behalf of the Tower.

The Constable takes part in various ceremonial occasions – here he is inspecting Yeoman Warders, before marching ahead of them to attend the state service. Lord Dannatt is very active with commentating politically and with his charity activities. He was also extremely helpful and supportive during the 'Poppies' project in 2014 (see part two). There is no doubt that his connections, dedication and skills have contributed significantly to the continuing success of today's Tower.

Lord Dannatt being interviewed for the media

Quirky question from a visitor:

Where is the tower where you make the Beefeater gin?[1]

Contributor: Yeoman Serjeant (Beefeater) Crawford Butler

---

[1] Some of the quips and anecdotes recounted in this book may appear to be disrespectful as well as amusing. There is no doubt that everyone involved with Historic Royal Palaces values and appreciates every visitor equally and respectfully. This specific, rich brand of humour has its roots in the pressures and adversity undertaken willingly by the armed forces on our behalf. It deserves to be savoured, enjoyed and appreciated – no offence is ever intended.

February 2015

February 7th 1812: Charles Dickens was born. One of the ravens at the Tower is named after his pet, Grip. In 2012, the Tower of London welcomed two new inhabitants: a pair of ravens named Jubilee and Grip. Their arrival celebrated the Queen's Diamond Jubilee and the bicentenary of Charles Dickens's birth. This Grip was the third of the Tower ravens to receive this name.

February 1st: Saint Peter ad Vincula Morning Service

Royal Military Police and the RAF attending this annual service

The congregation was joined by the Royal Military Police Association and the RAF for their annual services. Many other forces associations use St Peter ad Vincula similarly. The form varies – veterans wear their medals and some gather with their families and friends in the chapel, while others parade and march behind their regimental colours across the Broadwalk, processing to the Chapel. The service begins and if they have brought their colours, these are marched by their standard bearers to the altar and draped across it by the Chaplain, to remain for the duration of the service. Afterwards, the colours are marched out. On some occasions, veterans then parade outside the Queen's House, for inspection by the Governor or Constable. It is awesome to watch these spectacles. Younger relatives or partners may also wear the medals, but on the right breast, instead of the left. These people have a great sense of camaraderie and purpose, a reminder to us of the price people have paid and the need to honour and respect them.

Band leading the parade

Veterans back on the parade ground

Crawford Butler before retirement   *Medieval interior*

February 2nd

Yeoman Serjeant Crawford Butler agreed to show me up to the first floor of the Byward Tower, to see the only surviving decorated medieval interior at the Tower of London. It illustrates the crucifixion of Christ and is thought to date from the 1390s. Unfortunately, it is not accessible to the general public because of severe access and preservation difficulties. I felt privileged yet sad at not being able to describe this visual feast adequately or knowing how to share it with readers. However, thanks to modern technology, this problem is resolved – the BBC have recorded an excellent account. Please, find the time to see it at http://www.bbc.co.uk/programmes/p0215tvs.

February 5th: Interview with Yeoman Warder Jim Duncan

Jim was the lead representative of the Yeoman body for the recent Poppies project and says he was chosen probably because he had previous experience of the Royal Tournament. He describes himself as a doer; if a job needs doing, he'll get on and do it. His fuller account of the Poppies project can be found in Part Two.

Jim has been honoured for his work on Poppies and will receive his medal at Buckingham Palace (see November 17th).

Jim Duncan

He says:

> We are no longer military people, here at the Tower; we are all retired. At times, John or whoever puts on his bits and pieces and becomes deputy governor or whatever else he is doing; same with the Constable and Dick Harrold, the Governor. Then they become sir and all that sort of stuff, but when they come into the Yeoman's Bar or wherever, he'll be calling me Jim and I'll be calling him John. But you'd be a fool if you didn't respect them for what they'd done in previous engagements.

February 6th: Gun Salute

There was a sixty-two-round gun salute today at 1pm to mark the anniversary of HM the Queen's accession to the throne. Why sixty-two? Twenty-one to celebrate the royal anniversary, a further twenty because the Tower is a Royal Palace and Fortress, then another twenty-one for the City of London. The number varies according to the occasion. The following events receive a similar treatment: 6th February (Accession Day), 21st April (the Queen's birthday), 2nd June (Coronation Day), 10th June (the Duke of Edinburgh's birthday), the Queen's official birthday (a Saturday in June), 14th November (the Prince of Wales's birthday), State Opening of Parliament (usually November or December), when Parliament is prorogued by the sovereign, on royal births and when a visiting head of state meets the sovereign. These salutes take place at the Gun Park, on Tower Wharf.

Yeoman Warders supervise the closure of the wharf at least one hour before the event; no access is then allowed until after the ceremony. Today, tension mounted as the time got nearer and Yeoman Warders reacted expertly with the gathering crowds, warning about the noise and smoke, handing out ear plugs to

Honourable Artillery Company

Ready to fire

those concerned. Guests are allowed to stand on the grass on the south side of the main entrance.

The gun convoy arrived loudly, suddenly and at considerable speed, so the Yeoman Warders were very alert (as always) to ensure that the viewers were safe and not in the way. Members of the Honourable Artillery Company looked spectacular as they roared onto the wharf and set up ready on the Gun Park. When prepared, the crews were brought to attention by their senior officer.

This was all watched over vigilantly by Yeoman Gaoler and, when satisfied, the Chief Yeoman Warder signalled, then the parade was joined by the Constable, Governor and Deputy Governor. Then came the Royal Salute, with smoke gradually building up as shell after shell was fired – the tension was incredible, as people stopped to reflect, or struggled with the booming noise (it's still surprisingly loud, even when braced and ready).

It gets very loud

The history, spectacle and symbolism – what a show – and it's free!

The convoy dispersed as rapidly as it had arrived, and within minutes Tower Wharf was back to business as usual and the Yeoman Warders could change back from their heavy state uniforms to their lighter ordinary wear.

Crowds watching the salute

Guns leaving

Public and soliders watching the salute

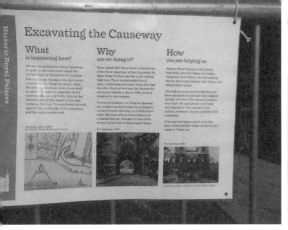

Repairs and excavation work explained

Panelling for renovation work

February 9th: Archaeological Excavation and Renovation Work

Major upheaval was being caused by the need for archaeological excavation and resurfacing on the Causeway, leading from the main entrance and including the normal congregating area for the Yeoman Warder tours. In my enthusiasm, I lingered to see what was going on but was soon told to hurry along because it was important to keep the newly congested area clear for the constant number of visitors passing through. This gave an extra headache to gate staff and Yeoman Warders, having to divert incoming visitors through a much narrower space, urging them to move quickly to avoid congestion. These initiatives are important both to preserve for the future and to learn more about the past. Bear in mind that HRP is an independent charity, which raises all its own funds. This means that our national treasures are looked after without cost to the country.

The pictures below show the extent of the renovation work of the Queen's House undertaken during 2015. Clever use was made of a false façade, which will come as a surprise to some regular visitors; from a distance, it was difficult to tell that it wasn't real.

Back of Queens House being renovated

The clever false façade

Excellent flower arrangement

Alan Kingshott

Governor, Chief, Constable, Gaoler

February 15th: Saint Peter ad Vincula Morning Service

Today's sermon in the Chapel Royal was given by Revd Chris Kellock MA BD CF, Chaplain, First Battalion, the Royal Regiment of Fusiliers. He had just returned from Sierra Leone with the Armed Forces Group and spoke about the work there to combat Ebola. They had set up and run a specialist field hospital, working under appalling conditions (not least because of the temperature and restrictions caused by the protective clothing, where a single careless mistake could lead to personal contamination). He said:

We gathered at each survivor's discharge to cheer, clap, sing and, yes, even to offer our prayers of thanks to God. It was a humbling time for us all as we handed the individual their Ebola survivor certificate.

February 17th: Interview with Chief Yeoman Warder Alan Kingshott

Alan: As far as ceremonies are concerned, we have lots, as you can imagine. There are some ceremonies which take place outside regular working or opening days, for example, the new Yeoman Warders when they swear allegiance; that happens at six o'clock when the public have left. We have the Beating of the Bounds, again at the end of the day because it goes outside the Tower grounds, so people who are there on the day get to see it. [See May

14th for more information on the Beating of the Bounds.] On the 21st of May every year we have the Ceremony of the Roses and Lilies, which takes place at 6.30. So a lot of the things we do remain closed to the public, except by invitation or when we go outside the Tower. There are one-offs that come about once every three or five years and the one big one, which is the installation of the new Constable: it will be as big a ceremony as you'll get at the Tower – it takes a lot of organisation, lots of people are invited, including many VIPs. Having said that, 2014 was exceptional, because of the poppies; we had ceremonies that took place on an ad-lib basis. As the popularity of Poppies grew, the interest of VIPs increased … we were having to plan for some visits with only about 30–45 minutes' notice. There were lots of impromptu sorts of ceremonies.

On the occasions when the Queen visits, the rule is for everybody to be in state dress and we generally get to have a photograph with her. She does not like to disrupt the normal running of the establishment, so we were able last year to have half the Tower open. The people who came in that day could see cars being driven through and were saying, 'Who is it? My gosh, it's the Queen!' Since I have been at the Tower, Her Majesty has formally visited three times. On each occasion there is a photograph with all of the Yeoman Warders; her first visit I was in the back row, second visit, the middle row, then in November 2014 I was in the front row.

The Chief leading the Band of the Royal Marines

I am to retire at the end of March 2017, not because I'm fed up with the job, it's absolutely brilliant, but I just want to enjoy another phase in my life. I want to go off and do something else; there are other challenges that I and my wife, who has retired from working in the Jewel House, wish to explore. So we will probably do presentations to schools and similar, that's our plan, but we shall see how it goes.

In the future, I don't think we'll stop, but it will change dramatically, I think. As Yeoman Warders, we need to modernise; we need to share the stories about some of our hidden ceremonies. It's something we're in the process of doing right now, trying to bring everybody up to date in today's world. There are lots of things around the Tower that will be IT-led and I think that we need to do more storytelling and less of the old-fashioned stuff that we were responsible for when I first got here∎

February 22nd: Saint Peter ad Vincula Morning Service

It being the first Sunday in Lent, Canon Roger addressed the symbolism of the True Cross, as well as the purple robe of mockery, the nails, the crown of thorns, dye that soldiers used to cast lots for Christ's robe, and the sponge set on a reed to offer gall and vinegar to Jesus. He also announced that the Bishop of London would again be conducting a service of confirmation in the Chapel Royal. There were already three candidates and any more would be welcome.

As Dean of the Chapels Royal, the Bishop of London has significant historical and religious duties to honour at the Tower, as well as his own pastoral interest and his interest as a historian. He says:

Symbolism of the True Cross

The Implements of Mockery

It being a Royal Palace, I'm there not as the Bishop of London, but as Dean of Her Majesty's Chapels Royal; I'm always addressed in the Tower as Mr Dean. So, in a way, I'm not responsible to myself as Bishop, so I can be wild! But of course, wildness as far as I'm concerned means being able to be even more conservative than I am usually!

February 26th: The Wave and Weeping Window
                 on Tower Wharf

Interestingly, these iconic symbols that became world-famous as part of the Poppies sculpture have been stored here for some time without attracting attention, after being dismantled after Remembrance Day 2014. The Poppies are carefully wrapped up for protection from the weather, which also makes them difficult for passers-by to recognise. Plans are under way for them to be featured in displays around the country until 2018, after which they will be on permanent display at the Imperial War Museum.

Iconic poppy symbols stored unrecognised on Tower Wharf

February 28th: How Do the Ladies Fare?

Pauline Dodd is married to Yeoman Warder Simon Dodd and was Operations Manager with a private health company when she moved into the Tower. She had always lived in her own house and had no experience of 'army life' because Simon would come and go daily, or at the end of a tour of duty. With a successful nursing and management background, she was tough and well-disciplined, yet it was a big new learning curve and hard work adapting to life at the Tower.

I think my main worry when I first arrived was feeling controlled and entrapped. It has to be monitored because you've got the Crown Jewels, etc. of course, but it took time to get used to. The hardest thing for me in the first few nights was that claustrophobia because I didn't realise that someone could open the gates. I thought I'm stuck in here, can't leave, and didn't know that you just need to ask and you can get out – being new I just didn't know. I couldn't understand issues here related to the army and I had nothing to compare it with because I've had nothing to do with the military. I was grateful not to commute but very challenged by leaving my home, so it took me a while to really become comfortable. Yeah, I was brand new.

One very close friend is Julie, Gaoler's wife. Chris was Simon's mentor and I met Julie before we even moved in here because they invited us over for a barbecue. I think for me we just hit it off and have been friends ever since. Chris is also a lot of fun, he and Simon are friends and, believe it or not, we never talk about this place. Julie and I catch up outside at the café on the wharf, or if the Tower is closed we'll sit on the wharf itself, or go to St Katharine Docks for a coffee there, or go for a walk.

To me, this is a rental in London in a fabulous location, where I know my car won't be stolen and my house will not be broken into, so I can sleep very comfortably. I've got a huge number of positives with being here because, you know, I don't need to worry. I am very strict that family comes to my house, not the Tower; it is my home and not a museum and is the best that I can make it. It's about living a normal family life here. I think I'm lucky and very privileged.

Simon was a warrant officer in the Grenadier Guards before coming to the Tower. He did guard duty at Spandau Prison and is a great fisherman.

Pauline Dodd, Yeoman Warder's wife

I have gained the impression that living in the confined, small area can be lacking in privacy, and coming to terms with the security and necessarily strict rules can initially be difficult. The probationer arrives six months earlier, so has already established familiarity and friendships, whereas everything is completely new for the partner on arrival. The Tower being such a unique, high-profile place to live, family members need to learn quickly about discretion and not to talk about certain issues. Care seems to be taken to ensure privacy within the home and 'rental' is quite different to ownership. The forces' banter can be difficult to get used to – there seems to be agreement that you need to learn to laugh with it and give back as good as you get. Getting in and out may be irritating at busy traffic times (particularly during 'Poppies').

On the positive side, there is great appreciation for the privilege, safety, prestige and other advantages of living in the Tower. One lady commented that the nature of people's back-grounds is very diverse, so it is easy to find others with similar interests. There seems to be a good community spirit, with people caring for each other, supporting new arrivals and never needing to feel alone. The ladies have their own annual function and also attend the two dinner events each year. New Year's Eve is an all-time favourite.

Quirky question from a visitor:

Are the Crown Jewels kept on Tower Bridge?

Contributor: Jack Chrysanthou, staff member

March 2015

March 2nd 1101: Ranulf Flambard escapes from the Tower of London. The first person to be imprisoned within the Tower's walls, he was also the first to escape! Bishop Flambard was imprisoned in the White Tower by King Henry I. He invited his guards to join him for a Candlemas feast, having smuggled in a rope in a gallon of wine. Once the guards were drunk and asleep, Flambard used the rope to make his escape by climbing down the wall of the White Tower to safety.

Daffodils outside the main entrance

The leek in the hat

March 1st: St David's Day and the Daffodils Look Grand

Yeoman Warder Paul Cunliffe was a regimental Sergeant Major in the Welsh Guards. He comes from Rhyl in North Wales and proudly wears a leek in his hat to celebrate his country's patron saint. Further discussion led to him disclosing that he also flies his national flag outside his home and proudly wears a Welsh Guards sweatshirt.

Paul was severely injured while defending against the attack on the *Sir Galahad* troopship during the Falkland Islands Campaign. As a drill sergeant, he was chosen to lead the funeral cortege that

The Welsh Guards t-shirt   Flying the Welsh dragon

carried Princess Diana's coffin into Westminster Abbey. He said that on walking down the aisle, in front of his eight pall bearers, he could see people crying and the only way to get through it was to think of something totally different, so he just dwelt on thoughts about his favourite football team, Leeds United.

March 4th: Interview with Katie Newton, Site Facilitator, and Megan Gooch, Learning Producer

Katie: I look after the operational delivery for the children, so making sure that they are expected on site, have all the materials needed and know exactly where to go for the session that people like Megan have helped put together, and just making sure that everything is smooth-running. It is a big operation.

Professional actor engaging a young audience

Children at the Tower

Actors engaging young and old

Megan: My side is developing sessions for them to come and take part in, and Katie makes sure that they all have a fab time on the day. Previously as a curator, while researching the Mint at the Tower, I would bump into these costumed interpreters followed by gangs of children and think 'oh', and then, when I actually came to the department, I suddenly realised just how many children we have coming through every single day. The national curriculum has an effect on what we do. Luckily the Tower has a thousand years of history, so we can adapt quickly to changes made.

Katie: We need to reflect what the curriculum needs, so when changes are made we have to work really hard to build our resources up again, make it cross-curricular and try and think of different angles.

Megan: We point out that the Tower is not the most accessible place; it often takes people by surprise. They may imagine that it is like the British Museum, spacious, under cover, with plenty of places to sit. But most of it is out in the open, lots of cobbles, and once you are up in places like the White Tower, there is not much seating. If you are tired or have a dodgy knee, then it can be quite a journey, and if you have very young children you have to carry them about. We have a lot of school sessions where there is one child in a wheelchair or with some kind of particular need and we can accommodate them. Our classrooms are wheelchair-accessible; the people delivering the lesson can adapt it so they don't go up into the high wall walks. They can bring the past to life without having to go up a massive upper spiral staircase. We try and avoid them anyway because it's hard to marshal thirty-odd children and teachers. Everything takes time. Of course families with youngsters are equally important for us to consider as children on school visits.

We try to see the difference between happy children and disruptive children, which can sometimes be quite a fine line because they are both noisy. But really happy and engaged children are noisy in a more positive way. It is about learning to recognise that. Sometimes it can be quite intimidating to have thirty teenagers trooping on through, but having the skills to see if anything needs to be said and knowing which teacher to turn to means that we get relatively few problems.

Katie: Deliveries can be a nightmare. We had a delivery of Plastazote [conservation foam] that came on a pallet delivered by the East Drawbridge. We went to pick it up and we couldn't lift it; we got pulled over by the wind and fell over. So we got organised. To get anything delivered you need to know which entranceway, whether their van will fit, the vehicle dimensions, the driver's name and the vehicle registration, so we can get them in and think about where they are going to park. The children are much easier to organise!

March 8th: Tower Powerhouses Event

Starting at the Tower, this was an exciting new joint event, between London's Air Ambulance and Historic Royal Palaces. It involved seventy teams, being taken on a 5 km walk around the City of London. They had to follow clues and answer questions of historical interest. Everyone had a great time and £20,000 was raised, to be shared equally between HRP and London's Air Ambulance. The event will move to a new location in 2016: a 5 km route around Hampton Court Palace.

London's Air Ambulance close to the tower
Photograph: Matthew Bell

Another fine floral display

March 15th: Mothering Sunday. Saint Peter ad Vincula Morning Service

Canon Roger reminded us that Jesus asked John to take care of Mother Mary – children are entrusted to their mothers and similarly Mother Church is entrusted to future generations for the continuation of Christianity. He also reminded us that the Church 'is not shrinking'.

March 18th: Game of Thrones

The world premiere of *Game of Thrones* season five was screened at the Tower, three weeks before it was released in the USA. The red-carpet premiere was organised by Sky Atlantic.

The Director of Sky Atlantic in the UK, Zai Bennett, said:

Important premiere

> *Game of Thrones is the must-see show of the year and a massive show for Sky Atlantic, so I am delighted we will be hosting the world premiere of this epic show at the Tower of London. I can't think of a more fitting venue to give what promises to be another unmissable series its big launch.*

Considering the way in which the Tower is used for such promotions, I have listened to many different points of view about the best ways to utilise the Tower's historical moat. Traditionalists argue that it should remain unspoiled, local residents bemoan its ugliness following use by marquees, and others champion the facility for marketing and promoting 'today's Tower'. Maybe it's important to consider the excitement and straightforward joy for

Returfing is needed after the event

Marquee being erected

those able to visit the moat. Also, the much-needed revenue that it contributes for HRP, and (not least) when the marquees are removed, there is a period of muck and mud before the returfing, reminding us of 'after the poppies', of Flanders fields, of the 888,246 that we should never forget.

Resurfacing the grass for events like this is paid for by the marquee hirers – they work very quickly and this picture shows how it's done.

Relaying the turf

March 21st: End of an Era

Yeoman Serjeant Crawford Butler was chosen to lay the first poppy in the moat, being the longest-serving Yeoman Warder, among so many other successes. He had been helpful to me, providing information, pertinent suggestions and encouragement. Crawford struck me as a 'grand gentleman' with his mild-mannered, calm approach. The twinkle in his eye was always close and he regularly had me in awe of his humour and polished performance. (Incidentally, he wears an 'I support Liverpool' badge in his hat.)

Famous Liverpool supporters hat with it's 'support Liverpool' Badge

Delighted guests

My prized signed copy of limited edition poppies print

Crawford had agreed to allow me and a party of 'fellow historians' to join one of his renowned evening tours before the Ceremony of the Keys. I had already sought guidance and permission before approaching Crawford, not wanting to ask a favour just because of writing the book. It was one of only two personal favours asked (and granted). Then I heard that his retirement was imminent and was bitterly disappointed, which was unnecessary because, incredibly, Crawford allowed me and guests to join his final evening tour, to which he had invited his personal guests.

It was unforgettable – they always are, whoever is leading. But this was extra charged with a life of its own, due to it symbolising the best standards in hospitality and performance that Crawford could offer, given with his customary generosity and warmth – his tours coming to an end after an already distinguished army career, and a sparkling second one at the Tower.

The Yeoman Warders' Bar was a great delight to share with those who hadn't previously seen it, and I pulled my weight by helping to hand around the excellent fish and chip suppers. The Tower doesn't charge for these tours and attending the Ceremony of the Keys, so the only cost was for the food. We were invited to buy raffle tickets, to support the Yeoman Warders' own named charity. I was delighted to win a limited edition print of the Poppies, signed personally by Crawford, no less.

Delighted members of London Historians in the Yeoman Warders bar

March 29th: Palm Sunday

Led by Yeoman Warder Shaun Huggins carrying the Abyssinian Cross, Canon Roger, the choir and congregation process from the Fusilier Museum across the Broadwalk to the Chapel Royal, singing the traditional Palm Sunday hymn 'All Glory, Laud and Honour'. This gives a stirring start to the service and an extra spectacle for visitors and staff.

Quirky question from a visitor:

Which side of the river is Tower Bridge on?

Contributor: Bob Brown

Stirring start to the service

Palm Sunday procession across the broadwalk to St Peter's

April 2015

April 17th 1534: Thomas More is confined to a cell in the Bell Tower, part of the Queen's House at the Tower.

April 2nd: Maundy Thursday

Confirmation service in St Peter ad Vincula at six o'clock. Canon Hall conducted the service and the Bishop of London confirmed six members of the congregation – four adults and two younger members.

The Reverend Cortland Fransella undertook the preparation classes for the confirmation and says:

The four adults confirmed today neatly illustrate our diverse nature, coming from widely different backgrounds and even different continents. All were united in their wish to be confirmed in the Church of England – a personal and public declaration of their faith in Jesus Christ as their Lord and

St. Peter's ad Vincula

Saviour. In the preparatory sessions, we touched on a range of faith questions, the nature of the Church, the meaning of the Creeds, of Holy Communion and of confirmation itself. In any congregation, some are cradle Christians, others have come from different traditions and denominations, some are church-goers by habit and others are quite new to the faith – the congregation at the Tower is no different. After the confirmation service in St Peter ad Vincula we went to the ancient Chapel of St John's in the White Tower for the traditional Maundy Thursday service of Holy Communion. The newly confirmed received the wafer and wine for the first time, in a chapel which has been a place of Christian worship since the year 1078. Thus, amidst ancient liturgy and unaccompanied choral singing, we sensed that union in both time and space which is at the heart of Holy Communion, and of our congregation itself.

Inside St. Peter's ad Vincula

Holy Communion was at seven o'clock in the ancient St John's Chapel, with the Bishop of London, as Dean of the Chapels Royal. He says:

It is a very atmospheric place, high up in the White Tower. The acoustics are marvellous and our choir, of course, sings to extraordinary advantage. It has great spiritual density. It is the most wonderful Romanesque ecclesiastical structure, I think, in the whole of London, and ought to be much better known. This was the private oratory of the ruler. And so we go there after dark every Maundy Thursday. Roger introduced the risky custom of getting people to take off their socks and shoes and washing some feet, which of course is a very powerful way of recalling the events of the first Last Supper. It couldn't be a more resonant and haunting place in which to recall the night in which He was betrayed, where He ate supper with his friends. And so around that stone altar we gather and sing a hymn, as they did, of course, at the Last Supper. And then in preparation for Easter the altar is stripped and Psalm 22 is chanted, which includes so many of the pictures and images which are then incorporated in the crucifixion story. One of the great climactic experiences of the year is to go there, to the Chapel of St John. And I'm very glad that after some period of controversy as to whether St John, like St Peter, was in fact a Chapel Royal, we have managed to establish that it is.

Ancient St John's Chapel

April 3rd: Good Friday. Liturgy of the Cross: Faure Requiem and Good Friday Reflections

Sacristan Bernard

A fine performance at St Peter ad Vincula at 7pm, deeply appreciated by the audience for this solemn occasion.

Sacristan Bernard Jackson has been associated with the Tower since 1968 and he is responsible for keeping safe the vestments, furnishings, sacred vessels and records. Currently, for state service occasions, the 'Salver and Flagon' (normally displayed in the Jewel House) are placed on the altar. The Sacristan used to use the Salver regularly to hold the filled collection plates, prior to presentation to the officiating priest; it is very beautiful and he regrets its removal.

Deeply respected, Bernard has an incredible memory and eye for detail and is an accomplished expert on the furnishings and statues. He noted that on one of the Queen's visits, she was wearing the brooch that Prince Albert had given to Queen Victoria on their wedding day in 1840. Bernard recalls the Constable being fascinated by his collection of Maundy Thursday coins and this picture shows them in deep conversation. One important recollection was when Prince Charles attended a private communion service in St John's on his twenty-first birthday, accompanied by the Queen Mother and his sister, Princess Anne.

Bernard with the Constable

He regularly cycles to the Tower from his home in Euston; unfortunately, his previous bicycle was stolen, but the authorities presented him with a replacement.

April 5th: Easter Day. State Parade, Saint Peter ad Vincula Morning Service

The Governor

Today's state parade was led by the Governor, Col. Harrold, bringing a great end to Easter Week at the Tower. Special guests were members of the British Korean Veterans Association.

The font (c. 1350) made an impressive vessel for the Calvary scene and floral displays were excellent. Easter eggs were offered as the congregation filed out of the chapel.

This font was discovered during the 1876 restoration, when the Cholmondeley sarcophagus in the centre of the chapel was opened. It contained no bodies, but found inside was the font which now stands by the west door. It appears to have been hidden there by the then-chaplain to preserve it during the Commonwealth (when Cromwell ruled the country as a republic), but the priest presumably didn't tell anyone prior to his death, so the hiding place was unknown for over 200 years.

The ancient font

Many veterans return every year

Following the service, veterans paraded to the Queen's House, to be inspected by the Governor. The looks of appreciation and smiles are a reminder of the importance of these occasions – very moving to witness.

April 7th: Arrival of New Probationer Gary Thynne

The latest probationary Yeoman Warder, Gary Thynne, arrived to start his six months' training, sporting a beard envied by many of his colleagues. Gary, still a young man, has passed through his twenty-two years' good conduct and achieved senior rank in the Royal Artillery as Welfare Warrant Officer for two of their regiments. Though he is no doubt well prepared, now comes a gruelling period of concentrated, focused training as a probationer. For six months he will be immersed in learning 'the story'. During this time, he must live alone at the Tower, away from his wife. I gather that colleagues are very supportive and one of the Yeoman Warders is assigned as mentor. During this period, he will be transformed into a polished, entertaining, expert specialist performer and speaker on the history of the Tower of London, continuing with and adapting all the skills developed during a successful military career. Along the way he will also learn to live and breathe the twenty-one daily duties. A couple of weeks later, I observed that he was already charming the visitors. After mentioning his beard, he knows exactly how to crank up the amusement when he dramatically removes his hat!

Much envied beard

Qualifications to become a Yeoman Warder: *Achieve rank of Warrant Officer, Class 1 or 2 (or equivalent) in Royal Navy, Army, Royal Air Force or Royal Marines. Must have served a full career of twenty-two years, and hold the Long Service and Good Conduct Medal.*

Hairstyle revealed

April 9th: Yeoman Warder David Coleman Tour

Yeoman Warder David Coleman is the archivist and does chapel duty. I followed him around while he was conducting a tour. Irritatingly, a helicopter appeared overhead and sounded thunderous – it hovered above for at least twenty minutes. I mentioned this to several others, who were equally annoyed and deeply sympathetic towards David. He simply continued addressing the 200 or so people while appearing to not even notice the noise. When I asked him about it afterwards, he just shrugged his shoulders and smiled – marvellous! Unshakeable.

Duty as required

April 21st: Gun Salute to Mark the Queen's Birthday

The Queen has been on the throne for more than sixty-three years and on September 9th she will overtake Victoria to become the longest-reigning monarch in British history. The Queen is spending the day privately at Windsor Castle.

The Queen's official birthday will be in June. The tradition of two birthdays dates back to the time when, if monarchs were born in winter, the weather was deemed unsuitable for outdoor events.

Royal gun salute

Gaoler and escort

Parading the cask

April 27th: Ceremony of the Constable's Dues

This ancient custom re-enacts the collection of tax payable to the Constable. Nowadays brandy, rum or wine is used and it is marched through the Tower in a keg carried on an oar, the band-led guard having been first formally refused, then given permission to enter. The procession then makes its way along Water Lane and threads around to the Broadwalk and finally onto College Green. The keg is ceremoniously handed over to the Constable to pay the 'dues', then officers withdraw to the Queen's House for sustenance, while more junior ranks are invited to the Yeoman Warders' Club. This time it was the turn of HMS *Defender*'s Commander and ship's company, led by the Band of HM Royal Marines. Officers were entertained by the Constable and Governor, while other ranks were well looked after in the Yeoman Warders' Club.

Further information about the event is available at: londonhistorians.wordpress.com/2015/04/27/the-ceremony-of-the-constables-dues/ and a film at https://www.youtube.com/watch?v=5h59fNIFfkE.

March past

Chief, **HMS Defender's Commander**, *Constable, Deputy Governor*

Saluting for the band of the Royal Marines

The Poppies Installation

April 29th: HRP Wins Two Major Awards.

Historic Royal Palaces won two major awards for 2015, from the Museums + Heritage Awards scheme, which is considered the 'Oscars' of the museums and heritage sector. Chief Executive Michael Day was presented with the award for **Outstanding Contribution by an Individual**, while the Poppies installation at the Tower of London, *Blood Swept Lands and Seas of Red*, won the **Best Temporary or Touring Exhibition** award.

About the Poppies installation, the judges remarked:

> *Risk-taking, brand-stretching, game-changing, the most significant example of a secular pilgrimage in the modern age, this is a project which symbolises the nation's engagement with the First World War and one which will undoubtedly have a long-lasting legacy.*

Quip:

What's it like working here? Well, it's better than being shot at!

Contributor: Yeoman Warder Jason Woodcock

May 2015

May 19th 1536: Anne Boleyn, Queen Consort, is beheaded on a scaffold in front of the White Tower after being convicted of adultery, incest and high treason.

May 6th: British Heart Foundation, Thirty-Seventh Annual
Health Run

Back for its thirty-seventh year running, this fun run is well organised and the moat is greatly appreciated by participants of all ages. As the organisers say:

> Choose from distances of 5 and 10km, set your own pace and experience this incredible event with your friends, family or colleagues. The 1km route is all on grass and although mainly flat can be slightly uneven in some sections.

I spent some time down in the moat, talking with people and listening to many different comments; participants seemed as thrilled about visiting the moat as they were by the achievement involved with running and raising money for the charity. The skilled guy doing the commentary kept encouraging people forward and everyone was dedicated, regardless of fitness level. The onsite medics reassured me that despite huge numbers running over the years, remarkably few mishaps were recorded and those were only minor.

Fun and fitness in the moat

The White Tower

May 6th: From Forest to Fortress

Work started on the new White Tower steps (see October 22nd for the full story). The world-famous White Tower was built to awe, subdue and terrify the population and to defend against invaders. High up in the Tower is the ancient chapel.

Bishop Richard comments:

> *The White Tower, which of course as we know was built by Gandulf, Bishop of Rochester, was a place where the young sprigs of the nobility used to watch over their arms overnight, because that's where the Knights of the Bath (which had absolutely nothing to do with the order revived by Sir Robert Walpole as a nice little earner at the beginning of the eighteenth century) were bathed close by and then went to look over their arms in St John. I think we did something here, years ago, about the Knights of the Bath. I discovered that, as so very often, the truth was that you had to tip the man who looked after your clothes, the person who ran the bath water, and at every stage there was a payment to be made!*

May 14th: Ascension Day

The Beating of the Bounds ceremony takes place on Ascension Day every three years, and the last one took place in 2014. Though not current, I include it here because it is important and not well enough known.

The Beating of the Bounds ceremony involves Tower residents and local children, who beat out the boundaries of the Tower of London with willow sticks in an ancient and colourful ceremony. It begins with an Evensong service in the Chapel Royal. Then the Governor, Chief Yeoman Warder and Chaplain lead the procession of Yeoman Warders, choir, residents and staff members to Tower Hill. The Chief Yeoman Warder instructs the children that when he says 'roar', he means **roar loudly**! On arrival at the first marker, he roars, 'Mark well,' instructing the children to beat the marker with willow wands and reply with a cry of 'Marked'.

Beating the Bounds

The procession continues up the hill, until it is met by the parish party of All Hallows. The Resident Governor announces the ceremony of Beating of the Bounds to the Vicar of All Hallows and assures him that they come in peace, before both parties doff their hats and the procession marches through the parish party. They then continue across the main road, eastwards along the boundary and back across the road, down St Katharine's Way, marking and roaring along the way, then back into Tower Wharf and into the Tower, finishing with a rousing rendition of the national anthem.

Chief Alan comments as follows:

> *The beating of the bounds last year was fantastic, that was my first one as Chief; I was able to go out to one of the local schools in Upminster, to purloin fifteen of the kids – they were brilliant. Two of my little grandchildren were here, Evie and Ethan. Both were given great big long sticks four times as big as themselves; they wanted to hit the bounds with great enthusiasm of course. The children from the school, they gave them lots of room and encouraged them; they had a lot of fun. It was a moment for the children to be part of the history of the Tower and they will remember that for a long, long time.*

I was near the front and it was a big mistake not taking ear plugs! The looks on people's faces were a picture to behold – I saw amazement, astonishment, wonder, disbelief, pride and thrill (not to mention fury from delayed motorists).

An excellent description of the 2011 Beating the Bounds is on the 'Spitalfields Life' blog:

http://spitalfieldslife.com/2011/06/06/beating-the-bounds-at-the-tower-of-london/

*Floral tributes arrive at the
Execution Memorial*

May 15th: Floral Tributes on Anniversary of Anne Boleyn's Execution

Numerous flowers arrived at the Tower of London to mark the anniversary of Anne Boleyn's execution. Following public display on the Execution Memorial, the bouquets were laid inside the Chapel Royal, reverently close to the altar, where her remains are buried.

I mainly focus on 'life at the Tower' in this book because there are numerous history books about the Tower. However, I digress here to say more about the Execution Memorial because the depth of its inspiration is often overlooked. The link offered below explains more thoroughly.

> *The sculpture is by British artist Professor Brian Catling and the circular memorial focuses on the ten executions that have taken place on Tower Green, within the castle's walls. The following link provides further explanation.*
> http://www.culture24.org.uk/history-and-heritage/royal-history/art39959

Anne Boleyn was Queen of England from 1533 to 1536 as the second wife of King Henry VIII.

May 17th: Saint Peter's ad Vincula Morning Service

The regular service was given an extra treat by welcoming members of neighbouring HMS *President*, coinciding with the hundredth anniversary of Gallipoli. A moving account was given of how Sub-Lieutenant Tisdale won his Victoria Cross, the highest award for valour. He had been a serving officer with HMS *President* and relatives were present, visiting London specifically to take part in the Gallipoli Memorial Commemoration in Whitehall.

Commander John Herriman, Commanding Officer of HMS *President*, quoted from the official citation stating:

Beautiful floral display next to the Abyssinian Cross

> *Sub-Lieutenant Arthur Tisdale was killed on the 9th May 1915 during the landing on 'V' Beach at Gallipoli. Hearing that some wounded men were on the beach calling for assistance, he jumped into the sea and, pushing a dinghy in front, went to their rescue. In all, he made four or five trips to the beach and many men were saved. Under heavy and accurate fire from the Ottoman forces, he was shot and killed. For this gallant act and heroic bravery, Lieutenant Tisdale has been awarded the Victoria Cross, posthumously.*
>
> *There were two branches of the Tisdale family together, who hadn't met for decades because they had gone off in different directions. They had travelled from all over – I think some from around the world – to be here for the commemoration. So we attended that service, which was very special, and then we brought them back here to President for a small reception, which was easy to do and they could look around where their ancestor had served. They laid out a family tree on the table so they could see where the two branches of the family had gone their different ways. It had been quite unexpected for them and they were honestly amazed at being given such privileged access to the service at the Tower. Yes, it makes us feel good as a unit, but it was actually about them, and it was lovely to be able to do it.*

HMS President

May 20th: Interview with the Constable

Builders were extensively renovating the outside of the Queen's House, which is the Constable's residence at the Tower of London. He was very pleasant and informal while brewing a timely cup of tea, before I followed him into the drawing room. There we both sat comfortably, though under the watchful eye of his great predecessor, the Duke of Wellington, thanks to the famous picture hanging close by. Lord Dannatt remarked that it would all be rather splendid if only we weren't in a plastic bag, looking out across the Thames to Boris's Bunker. He had already got me smiling by welcoming me to 'this remarkable historic building site', observing that early that morning, builders had seemed so close he had thought they might be joining him in bed.

We began our interview by discussing the need for continued fundraising efforts by the Tower.

The Constable

St Peter ad Vincula

As Constable, I chair the Constable's Fund, our benevolent fund within the Tower. What I discovered over my first couple of years in the role, however, was that the fund didn't have enough money to do all the things it needed to. The choral foundation was not able to pay the costs of the choir and the chaplain also felt very strongly that the chapel of St Peter Vincula, as a Chapel Royal, needed a lift regarding its appearance. What I said, therefore, was, 'Let's combine these aspirations into one, let's have an appeal to correct these issues.' Then a third aim developed, which was to sort out the crypt where Thomas More is buried, so that we could better tell his story – a compelling British history story. The target was £1.5 million. Lots of people did lots of things, asked lots of people for money, laid on various events. By the 1st of October last year, we had met our target; we were then actually able to overachieve through the generosity of one particular person, and the total raised was £1.7 million in the end. Some of the things we did here in the house were particularly aimed at raising money for the chapel appeal. One example is on a variety of state occasions we fire gun salutes on the wharf. This is an excellent opportunity to invite people to come and watch, then have lunch in Queen's House, followed by a tour, a visit to the crypt and a visit to the Crown Jewels. That sort of invitation to people made it much easier than to say, 'Would you like to contribute to our appeal?'

Talk then turned to the Tower's Christian heritage:

I think the Christian faith, with all its vicissitudes through history as far as England and the United Kingdom is concerned, is very much part and parcel of the Tower of London's story. Sir Thomas More was held in the cell downstairs for the last fifteen months of his life and very much sums up that tussle between accepting Catholicism and the supremacy of the Pope, and the way in which Henry VIII wished to take the church. More now being buried in the crypt in the chapel, I think, shows how close the Tower has been to the development of Christianity and understanding of the place of the Christian faith in our nation's life.

At the end of national service, the Tower stopped being a military garrison and the Royal Fusiliers depot closed. There was a view at the time that the chapel would just become more museum space, but then the choral foundation started, the chaplain was appointed and the chapel continued. I think it surprises people that there is a vibrant chapel community here in the Tower of London. Some residents of the Tower attend, though most of the congregation come from outside. I think that's a fine way of connecting the Tower with the wider community.

This coming Sunday is the Whitsun state service; I should be here for that and I'm very happy to dress up with my feathers and sword and march at the head of the Yeoman body across to the chapel. I relate very much to the Yeoman body and feel that I understand them – thirty-seven of them, all ex-military. Though predominantly from the army, amongst them we have two Royal Marines, five Royal Air Force and one from the Royal Navy ... Because they are an extended part of the royal household and I'm a royal appointment, they see me as a sort of pastoral boss. I pass the time of day, chit-chat with them. I swear them in. They're a great bunch; we all get on very well, as you would expect old soldiers to do.

It's a five-year appointment as Constable, and it looks like I'm going to do seven, the way it's turning out. My wife and I have thoroughly enjoyed it because it's a fascinating and enjoyable place to be. I'd like to think we made a bit of a contribution through the chapel appeal and some role in Poppies.

Lady Dannatt also contributes a great deal in her own right. She passionately enjoys the history of the Tower and the Queen's House and hosts the more formal meals and receptions with her husband, often acting as knowledgeable tour guide. She is extensively involved in opening the Queen's House for many school and family groups, showing a particular interest in visits by children with mental health difficulties. There is a large kitchen, which the Dannatts also use for themselves, and I was privileged to look around in there. On the walls are a myriad of thank-you letters from a whole host of different-aged children, often featuring the two Norfolk terriers which are important members of the Dannatt family; they express the depth of gratitude that these children and their parents and teachers feel. Choir members comment that Lady Dannatt and her husband both take a keen interest in the music and their work, and numerous members of the community have mentioned her in conversation with affection, appreciation, love and respect.

May 21st: The Ceremony of the Lilies and Roses

This famous annual event is held in the Wakefield Tower and attended by the provosts of Eton College and King's College, Cambridge. They pay homage to King Henry VI, who founded both their colleges, by laying their college emblems (lilies and roses respectively) on the spot where the King was allegedly murdered on the 21st of May, 1471. Invitations are limited because of the confined space, so I greatly appreciated my own invitation.

Wakefield Tower

Treasured invitation

Choir hurrying to form up for the procession

Throne in the Wakefield Tower

We gathered in the Jewel House before the ceremony and processed from there at twilight. We were preceded by the Abyssinian Cross, with choir in scarlet, Chief Yeoman Warder and colleagues in ceremonial dress, Sacristan Bernard in white, Canon Roger in one of his finest robes, Governor Colonel Harrold in tail suit, provosts in university gowns and the young Etonians in their traditional tail suits with wing collars. This colourful procession wound its way along Water Lane, up narrow steps, across a stone bridge and through a low doorway into the octagonal chamber, filling the room, adding to the dignity and solemnity of the occasion. The short service was led by the Chaplain, with first his words and then the choir's plainsong reverberating around the chamber, followed by the formal laying of the lilies and roses on the spot where King Henry was allegedly slain while at prayer. A similar ceremony takes place at Windsor.

More information and pics at:
http://spitalfieldslife.com/2011/05/24/the-ceremony-of-the-lilies-the-roses-at-the-tower-of-london/

May 24th: Saint Peter's ad Vincula Morning Service, Whitsun State Parade

Today's parade was one of the three which take place each year; the others being Christmas and Easter. The Yeoman body wear their state dress with medals and the Constable (or Governor) wears his full-dress uniform. Following fortification at the Queen's House with a liberal measure of sherry, shared between members of the Yeoman body and the Constable (or Governor), Yeoman Gaoler orders his colleagues to collect their partisans, which have been left outside, and form up ready for inspection. When ready, he informs the Chief Yeoman Warder, who notifies the officer on parade that the escort is ready for review. The

Leaving weapons prior to entering The Queen's House

Inspection prior to the State Parade

Constable leaving his official residence

parade is then brought to attention and the Constable inspects the Yeoman Warders, escorted by the Chief Yeoman Warder. Then the Constable takes his place at the head of the parade, marching from the Queen's House to the Chapel of St Peter ad Vincula.

On arrival, the Constable is escorted to his seat by the Chaplain and the six Yeoman Warders then sit three each side of the aisle, while two end seats remain vacant for Gaoler and Chief Yeoman Warder. The choir and clergy then process to their places, led by the duty Yeoman Warder bearing the Abyssinian Cross. Then follows the marching down the aisle by veteran standard bearers (who hand their standards to the Chaplain, to be placed close to the altar), followed by Chief Yeoman Warder and Yeoman Gaoler, who hand over the silver mace and axe to the Chaplain; he places them on the altar for the duration of the service. After all have withdrawn to their seats, the service begins. The sight is spectacular and splendid, with so much colour, history and tradition.

Not every member of the Yeoman body is slim and sylphlike. The state dress is bulky and uncomfortable, on top of which, if moving while seated, careful attention needs to be given to the position of the long sword scabbard, which can move quickly and noisily. One unfortunate confided that he suffers from gout and finds it hard not to fidget, which makes wearing the scabbard fearsome.

May 25th: Interview with Yeoman Gaoler

Christopher Morton currently holds this colourful, historic office. As a knowledgeable authority on the post's history, he recalls how Gaoler used to be the senior position at the Tower, before the introduction of Chief Yeoman Warder. As Gaoler, he is to be seen carrying the axe on ceremonial occasions – it is actually a copy of the original (which resides in the Governor's office) and dates back to 1500. Gaoler Christopher has only carried the original once, on the occasion of the Queen's visit in October 2014.

Gaoler

Gaoler used to supervise VIP prisoners, who had to pay for their keep, so supplementing his income. He would accompany prisoners by boat to Westminster for trial – on their return, if guilty, the axe would point towards the prisoner, notifying Londoners accordingly. On important occasions, he watches over the Serjeants who supervise the Yeoman Warders, always alert and attentive, leaving the Chief free to attend to overall management, often guiding VIPs, dealing with timing and any fine tuning as necessary. His proudest recollection is sitting in the front rank for the traditional picture taken when the Queen visited recently.

Christopher is very clear about priorities; most important (after security, of course) is informing visitors, particularly through the organised tours. Then comes interaction with individuals, helping everyone to experience the most memorable visit possible; this includes the relentless answering questions, posing for photos and giving directions. He regards the third important priority as the maintenance of tradition and ceremony, and is adept at overseeing every small detail and setting standards by example. At the recent Whitsun State Service, Chief Yeoman Warder Alan was on leave, so the lead was taken by Yeoman Gaoler bearing the mace, with Yeoman Clerk Philip stepping up to shoulder his much-coveted axe. In the Chapel Royal, they both processed to the front to hand over their weapons to the Chaplain, who laid them on the altar for the length of the service. At the end they received them back, again in procession. Though both are well versed in drill, this was an unusual procedure in a very tight space and less familiar to Philip – no problem because of Christopher's easy ability to lead and guide his colleague. Extra seniority has its disadvantages; he felt it necessary to give up his volunteer gardening in nearby Bermondsey, not having the time when promoted to Gaoler, though he is now free to bomb off to his main home most weekends.

Gaoler, an authority on the post's history

He organises the Tower's own Poppy Appeal each year and they were thrilled to raise more than £30,000 in 2015, £8,000 of which was raised close to Tower Hill Underground Station, where he and colleagues were often to be seen in civvies when off duty. Many of the coins were stored for some time and developed a green discoloration. Christopher spends much of his free time at weekends cleaning them up, before banking them; he won't allow colleagues to help – one theory is that it helps him unwind and relax, having spent the entire week solving issues for Yeoman Warders. Last year's Poppy Appeal (2014) raised about £29,000, which was due to the Poppies event. The total for 2013, as an example of an average year, was £8,500. However, this year he had a head start with £10,500 already in the bank, being the coins collected by the poppy volunteers last year.

Two of his memorable VIP visitors were George Osborne, whom he found surprisingly pleasant, and Princess Anne (though arriving with half an hour's notice). At the time of writing, Christopher is looking forward to completing his twenty years of service at the Tower and modestly describes his contribution as but a grain of sand in the size and length of its historic life.

May 26th: HMS *President* Annual Ceremonial Divisions

HMS *President* paraded for its annual Ceremonial Divisions on the Broadwalk today. Led by a band of the Royal Marines, the parade marched from headquarters in nearby St Katharine's Way,

March past by members of HMS President

Marching from St Katharine's Way

Photos by Mr Kevin Poolman, Lieutenant Commander Tony Scott RNR and Serjeant Ross Tilly RAF

across St Katharine Docks and along Tower Wharf, entering the Tower at the Middle Drawbridge and forming up on the Broadwalk. An inspection was conducted by Rear Admiral Clive Johnstone CBE, Assistant Chief of the Naval Staff, accompanied by Captain Jeremy Stocker RNR.

Numerous awards and medals were presented, one of which was particularly poignant: Joel Perren, son of HMS *President*'s Midshipman Rob 'Reggie' Perren RNR, received his great-grand-father's Arctic Star medal for service in World War II.

Commander John Herriman, HMS *President*'s Commanding Officer, commented that they are very fortunate to be able to use the nearby Tower for their church services and parades. There is nowhere like the Tower because it has a huge pull and is a great place for families to watch the unit on parade, and also for the public to be able to watch as the Divisions march from St Katharine's Way through the docks and onto Tower Wharf. During his nineteen years' regular service with the Royal Navy it was routine to switch to another ship or shore estabishment every two to three years, but this is not the case in the RNR, where people stay attached to the same unit for their entire career. Amongst his ship's company now there are those who joined in the 1980s and who will have attended the annual parade every year. This is almost unique in the RN and leads to a tremendously strong feeling of ownership and pride in HMS *President*. The unit therefore has an incredible bond with the Tower as well as with the local community.

HMS President's Commanding Officer

May 27th: Gun Salute to Mark the State Opening
of Parliament

Quip:

The rack is an ingenious device for making short people into tall people.

Contributor: Yeoman Warder Andrew Lane

June 2015

June 14th 1381: After being besieged in the Tower by the uprising of peasants protesting against a poll tax, fourteen-year-old King Richard II rides out and quells the rebellion at Blackheath. Wat Tyler is killed in a scuffle with the Lord Mayor of London and his head paraded on a spike.

June 2nd: Gun Salute to Mark the Queen's Coronation

Veteran gunner

Veteran gunner Mike Paterson is founder of the London Historians Society. He served as a gunner in the Rhodesian Artillery, so understands all about shooting the 25-pounder gun he is pictured with here. Mike had come specifically to see the gun salute and I was intrigued by the passionate way in which he explained how the gun works. Looking around at the crowds, I wondered about the thoughts, memories and experiences being stimulated at this moment, from all these people, in this unique place.

Mike commented:

As a fortress and defender of London from foreign invasion and public insurrection, the Tower has always been bristling with ordnance. Even today you'll see old cannons everywhere. This more modern 25-pounder field gun, which sits on the Broadwalk in front of the Waterloo Block, was the workhorse of World War II. It bears the crest of the Honourable Artillery Company (1537), Britain's oldest working regiment, who to this day perform all royal gun salutes outside the Tower.

Ready to fire

Number of rounds to be fired

June 4th: Inauguration of Yeoman Warder Gary Thynne

Aware that the Yeoman Warders are rightly traditional and sensitive about their affairs, I was surprised and grateful to be allowed to witness this very private and prestigious ceremony, when they invite their newest colleague into their midst. As well as the Constable, both Governor and Deputy Governor were present. Gary swore his oath with Bible in hand and dressed in a smart lounge suit, custom forbidding him to wear his uniform for the occasion. After the ceremony, Lord Dannatt chatted with Gary's wife and then went back inside the Queen's House with Lady Dannatt, who had also been watching the ceremony.

As we walked from Tower Green to the Yeoman Warders' Club, I sensed that this was very similar to a major family occasion: camaraderie, bonhomie, celebration. At the club, Gary signed the Yeoman Warders' book, flanked by the Serjeants and Gaoler. The atmosphere was now getting heady – the Yeoman body was genuinely welcoming Gary into this traditional elite, which has been serving the monarch and HM Fortress and Tower of London for centuries.

Swearing in of the newest Yeoman Warder

Lord and Lady Dannatt share the moment with the sworn in Yeoman Warder's proud wife

Mission accomplished

Chief Yeoman Warder Alan would like to see this and numerous other ceremonies opened up for the public to witness, and he says:

Toast by the Chief

Signing the Yeoman Warder's book

Our new Yeoman Warders have to swear allegiance to Her Majesty in front of the Yeoman body. The story that's not told is that people don't see it, because it's a private affair like some other ceremonies. It's something which I've been trying to broaden out and to have filmed as part of a documentary. There are still traditionalists who don't want that to happen, but I think there's a story there, as with a lot of the ceremonies we do. I would like people to see what goes on and be part of it. So whether that happens in my time I don't know, but I'm certainly pushing because it is nice to have people watching that process and see what happens when they swear the ancient oath on Tower Green in front of the Yeoman body. The individual is dressed in a suit, although their uniform will be ready. They won't have the red and gold one, they have to wait – they carry on with their training and then, once we know they're going to make the probationary six-month period, we book them in to St James's Palace, and only when they've sworn allegiance there are they permitted to wear the red and gold uniform. Again it's a very private ceremony, very limited to numbers, simply because of the room size where they do the swearing.

June 7th: Saint Peter ad Vincula Morning Service:
            Blessed Margaret Pole

Another splendid floral arrangement

During the morning service Canon Roger gave an impassioned and powerful address about the extraordinary injustice and the complicated chain of adverse events that gradually led to the disfavour and famously gruesome end for Margaret Pole.

Canon Roger has many different roles. Apart from his royal and other outside duties, his door needs to be open for the Tower's residents and members of the growing congregation, with his services welcoming the widest range of guests. He is also to be seen regularly showing people around the Tower, though the post is officially only part-time. Roger's background embraced chaplaincy worldwide and it is only for the last few years that he has been home for Christmas, previously having worked with troops abroad. One of his posts was as the last army chaplain in the Hebrides. Currently, he also fits in pastoral care at a nearby school. Roger's passions for his faith, family, music, poetry and 'people' all contribute to his ministry.

Canon Chaplain of the Tower

Bishop Richard Chartres (as Dean) comments:

The Tower, I think, is, as far as ecclesiastical matters are concerned, a difficult environment because the relationships that build up within walls are very intense [I know this from many colleagues]. The chaplain has to be very shrewd, to be the friend of all but in the pockets of none. And I think the chaplain is well-advised to observe the naval custom that when you meet somebody, you take their rank, whoever they are. So if you're talking to the person who drains the moat, you're a moat drainer, or if talking to a constable, you're a constable. And I think that that is the right sort of tradition for a priest in those circumstances. I do think that Roger is doing a most splendid job. And of course, he does have this connection with young people outside the Tower, which I think is so valuable, to bring that kind of experience within the enclosure.

The Chaplain in front of his house

June 12th: MBE Award Announced for the Deputy Governor

Jeremy John Brown, Head of Operations and Security, HM Tower of London has been awarded an MBE from the civil list for services to World War I commemorations and charitable work in 2014. Col. John Brown is more than just 'right-hand man' to the Governor, Col. Harrold, because his boss is also heavily committed with his work as a director of HRP and managing the Banqueting House and Hillsborough Castle.

Col. John is at the sharp end of balancing the quality of 'customer experience' with the need for conservation and heritage. One of his main skills is said to be logistics – I can only guess at the complexity of the work involved, but a statement he made to me on that subject was, 'Well, that's what the army does.' He says:

John Brown, Deputy Governor

> *Change is essential to keep our offer relevant to visitors but often appears to be in conflict with the nature of the heritage. It doesn't have to be and I have greatly enjoyed the challenge of harmonising the two requirements and working within the HRP business model.*

Pauline Dodd said about his decoration for 'Poppies':

> *He was here nearly every weekend throughout all that time, working incredibly hard. I just think his decoration was so well deserved and I was delighted when I read that he'd got it. We hadn't heard properly and maybe he didn't want the word to go around; that's his humility.*

June 13th: Gun Salute to Mark HM the Queen's Eighty-Ninth Birthday

Yeoman Warders appear in state dress until after the salute, then change into the much more comfortable regular uniform. Talking about the Queen to several of them separately, I found they were all pleased to express their appreciation and respect for her; among descriptions used were 'awesome', 'caring', 'dedicated', 'incredible', 'great role model', 'she's our boss' – and 'best boss possible' came up several times.

Yeoman Serjeant Jim Duncan (recently promoted) has been honoured with an RVM in the Queen's Honours List. Jim had this to say about his own satisfaction for the part he played in Poppies. It relates to a volunteer helping to lay poppies in the moat.

The Queen outside HMS President

A guy got down on one knee, with a poppy in his hand, and said [to his companion], 'Would you do the great honour of marrying me?' She took the flower and on it was the ring; she hadn't noticed it at first. I thought, yes, there's another very poignant moment. All kinds of people, genders and races developed their relationships, and people were freely talking to each other and making friends together; for that alone, it was worth doing.

More is written about Jim on February 5th and in Part Two.

Jim amongst the poppies

June 14th: Saint Peter ad Vincula Morning Service

Today, the Reverend Cortland Fransella, assistant to the Chaplain, conducted the services. He assists Canon Roger Hall most weeks and regularly deputises for the Chaplain. Cortland has also set up the Chapel Royal's new website and works part-time at Lambeth Palace.

Chaplain Roger is also one of the Queen's chaplains and was today delivering a sermon for the Queen.

The Reverend Cortland Fransella

A member of the congregation describes her experience as a 'regular' in the following way:

> There is a warmth and intimacy hidden within the Chapel Royal of St Peter. To the tourist's eye, it's a treat nestling against the splendour of the mediaeval battlements and towers. Once inside, the welcome to all who visit and share in the services and concerts becomes quickly apparent. The members of the congregation are revealed for their warmth, humour and sense of family.
>
> I came across the chapel by chance when visiting a friend who was singing in the choir. Nearly three years on, nothing could have prepared me for the continual vibrancy of St Peter's, where the past is part of the present and where becoming a regular visitor has provided me with an unexpected sense of pleasure. The recognition of all those who have used it as a place of prayer and peace, the beauty of the interior, a professional choir of exceptional standard, the shafts of sunlight bursting through the windows together with the warmth of all those connected with St Peter's make this a timeless and unique place.

June 26th: Interview with Colm Carey, Master of Music, Chapels Royal, Tower of London

Colm Carey

Colm: Having the post of Master of Music in these Chapels Royal is such a great privilege. One couldn't wish for two more wonderful buildings in which to work on a regular basis. One of the many things I love about being here – and it's because of the intimacy of the buildings – is that there is an immediacy to our music making, which is hard to achieve almost anywhere else.

The one single thing that I try to do every time the choir sings in a service is to make sure the essence and heart of the music is conveyed to the congregation, so that through our role as musicians in the church we might enrich, and deepen, the wonderfully expressive liturgy we use in the chapel. For me, music crosses all barriers and it's a world that anyone can step into and, while there, be completely safe and nourished. It's a form of utopia, really. Great music has its own spirituality, and hearing beautiful music performed to a high level can, and should, be a spiritual experience. And this is why it's so important that we strive for a very high standard of music making.

In terms of the music we sing, I try to have as wide-ranging a repertoire as the circumstances will permit. Keeping a balance between music of different periods, styles and pieces that will push the choir, pieces that will broaden horizons for all the congregation, all the while bearing in mind that everything has to be appropriate for any particular Sunday, is a lot to juggle, but it's also fun. Performing Tudor music in a Tudor chapel is especially satisfying. There's something about the space in St Peter's that suits it so well – one can feel the grandeur of the music while also hearing the fine details, which so often get lost in bigger, more resonant acoustics. The size of the room keeps the choir on their toes as there is nothing to hide behind(!), and this demands a great deal of skill from the individual singers. And I am so fortunate to have a fabulous bunch of professional singers who are very committed to the place, and I'm very proud that they bring so much to the life of the chapel. We are also very lucky to have an outstanding organist in Christian Wilson, who is a master musician. It's a great team to work with.

It's also an extraordinary place to work because of the history – to be surrounded by some of the people who have shaped the way this island has grown! Of course, as Chapel Royal musicians, we are the living embodiment of a tradition that goes back hundreds of years. The Tower today is essentially a museum – a very good museum! But these small chapels, within the great complex of what makes up the Tower of London, are very much living organisms. They may be visited as museums by millions, but their heartbeat is as sacred spaces. And to be part of that is an honour ∎

Colm reflecting

Quip:

Previously known as Water Gate, it's another thing we had before America, though unlike theirs, ours didn't leak!

Contributor: Yeoman Warder Bill Callaghan

July 2015

A welcome for visitors

July 10th 1553: The first of Lady Jane Grey's nine days as Queen of England. On that day she arrived by river, to take up residence in the Tower with the Duke of Northumberland and his son, Lord Guildford Dudley, her husband. That evening they had a strong disagreement when she refused to name him King.

July 2nd: Interview with Yeoman Serjeant George Brodie

Serjeant George joined the RAF as a chef and amongst other successes has managed the four largest RAF hotels (manager is 'Caremaster' in RAF parlance). The Tower shrewdly harnessed George's catering experience when he was commissioned to oversee the refurbishment of the prestigious New Armouries Banqueting Suite and Café. The bare shell was handed over by the builders, before he spent sixteen months supervising the kitting out of the premises with everything from carpets and furniture to all the equipment necessary to make the unit functional. This was a good example of utilising the diverse skills available to the Tower by the Yeoman Body. George particularly enjoys his turn as Acting Gaoler when his senior colleague is away. Most of all, however, he relishes the contact with the public, particularly the tours (which the Serjeants all share with their colleagues), and can still project effectively, despite not having trained his voice parade-ground fashion like his contemporaries.

The excellent cafe

The Banqueting Suite

July 11th: Marriage of Kathryn Vagneur and Admiral Rory McLean

The marriage of Kathryn Vagneur and Vice Admiral Rory Alistair Ian McLean took place today in St Peter ad Vincula, of which Rory and Kathryn are congregation members. The Duke of York, who was Rory's pilot on HMS *Brazen*, attended and read a lesson. Music by the choir and organist was sublime. Champagne in the sunshine and a piper capped the celebration, followed by the couple's escape in a 1971 Mini Cooper S.

Glorious wedding

Stunning escape

Above left: *Proud moment*
Above right: *RAF Regiment Association*

July 12th: Morning Service: Special Guests, RAF Regiment Association

This is a proud time for Yeoman Serjeant Peter McGowran, as he and his brother Rob both served in the Royal Air Force Regiment. Pete was able to welcome not only his old colleagues to the Tower, but also Rob, who was bearing his branch's standard, *and* to march their parade up to the Chapel Royal for the service and then back again. Rob McGowran is third from the left in the right-hand picture.

July 17th: Harley Meets Morgan!

Quietly walking along Tower Wharf, my eyes nearly popped when I saw fifty-plus Harley-Davidson motorbikes roaring in through the East Gate. I watched, agog, as I could hear them making their way up the hill and onto the Broadwalk. All was well; Yeoman Serjeant Peter McGowran was there and smiling.

Well, why not? David Hutchinson belongs to the 1066 (topical) chapter of the 'Harley Owners Group', based in Sussex. Moreover, he is brother-in-law to Canon Hall, who had obtained permission for them to visit.

Harley Davidsons 'at ease' on the broadwalk   *Wow!*

This gathering must be unique

1066 chapter of the Harley owners group

David said:

> *Canon Hall gave us a fascinating insight into some of the Tower's history and we were privileged to be shown the renovations that had been carried out, including the crypt, which isn't normally open to the public.*
>
> *Then Serjeant Peter entertained us, by having a conversation with the ravens. He had a lot to do with them at one point and they know him well.*
>
> *On a previous visit, some of us gathered together for a photo around my brother-in-law's splendid Morgan (known affectionately as Mr Toad). This time, as we drove off, we were stopped from leaving at the gate. Most embarrassing: the volume and vibration of the assembled Harley exhausts had set off an alarm system, so we had to wait until we were given the all-clear. This was our third visit and we are not too sure whether we will be welcomed back!*

What a sight

My guess is that they have been forgiven.

July 22nd: Saint Peter's ad Vincula: Choral Evensong, Patronal Festival

Chief guest today was Cardinal Vincent Nichols, Archbishop of Westminster. He referred to St Peter ad Vincula in his homily, saying:

> *The building of our society as a stable foundation for its traditions of democracy, the rule of law, desire for peace and respect for all people, needs the best from everyone. May the freeing of Peter from his chains be a constant reminder to us of the strength to be gained when the truths of our own faith flow strongly in the mainstream of our society.*

The Cardinal relaxing over drinks and canopes

Choir members, congregation and Tower personnel enjoying the occasion

Chatting together on the lawn

His full homily can be found at http://www.thechapelsroyalhm-toweroflondon.org.uk/events/events-archive/cardinal-nichols/cardinal-nichols-at-the-patronal-festival-8433.php

Drinks and canapés were provided on the lawn following the service. The setting is ideal and the weather was kind, so the event developed a memorable 'party' atmosphere. Similar to the coffee events held after services at the end of each month, this worked well to enable clergy, choir members, Tower officials and other 'regulars' to meet together. It is fair to say that the congregation is growing and thriving in this unique place, with its duty to honour legal requirements and historical preservation while serving the needs of the Tower's community and its visitors, as well as the local community.

Professor Tony Mellows RIP

Professor Anthony Mellows, OBE, TD was Vice-Chairman of HM Tower of London Chapels Royal Foundation, working closely with Canon Hall on finance, management, policy issues and general advice. Sadly, he died early in 2016.

Greatly respected

Tony is respectfully mentioned here because he always wanted to see more communal gatherings and the one above was clearly one he enjoyed himself, as shown in the top left picture, where he is to be seen, standing on the left. Tony and his wife Elizabeth had worshipped at the Tower for more than forty years and his input was considered invaluable; he is sorely missed. A tribute is given on the Chapels Royal website: http://www.thechapelsroyalhm-toweroflondon.org.uk/events/events-archive/professor-anthony-mellows-rip

July 23rd–26th: Tudors at the Tower – Family Festival

This spectacular attraction was to illustrate life in the sixteenth century and give a snapshot of the preparations and celebrations for Anne Boleyn's coronation. It certainly drew huge crowds. Parents seemed as engrossed as their children – fun and

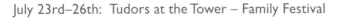

excitement was everywhere as I walked around. While the event was enjoyable and entertaining, people were also serious about learning and sharing the authentic value of what was on show.

As with other activities at the Tower, the actors involved take it very seriously and professionally; this is not 'second-rate' theatre, but playing an important part in telling the stories. The Yeoman body has perfected this and rightly remains central – they are what people come from all over the world to see, so the drama activities enhance this, adding a further dimension and encouraging visitors to come more often for the varying programme.

An HRP statement said:

> *Visitors were able to meet 'King Henry VIII and his new bride Anne Boleyn' at this family friendly festival in the Tower moat. It was filled with activities, recreating the sights and sounds of 1533 and people were able to dress up in the elegant Tudor costumes provided. There was candle making and Tudor cookery in hands-on workshops, while enjoying demonstrations from blacksmiths and carpenters as they prepared for the royal celebrations; even instruction on becoming 'the ultimate knight' and practice shooting a cross bow was available (very handy). A 'pop up palace' enabled families to take part in the interactive game staged virtually at Hampton Court Palace and to watch an Aardman animation film about Anne Boleyn's lavish coronation. The tiniest historians were entertained with special soft play areas for ages 0–5, with arts and crafts activities for all ages. Visitors could continue their visit inside the Tower walls at any time.*

Katie Newton said:

> *When we had 'Tudors at the Tower', there were lots of exciting things for families to do. We had dressing up and you couldn't get the adults out of the children's dress-up clothes. You had these moments when you had to go, 'Excuse me, madam, that's a child's costume.'*

> *Quip:*

> *While explaining the prisoners of the Bell Tower, during a special, I ask if anyone knows who 'The Man For All Seasons' was. To which, a tourist (out to impress his girlfriend) shouts out, 'Vivaldi!' Yeoman Serjeant Crawford Butler*

August 2015

August 23rd 1305: Having been sentenced to death, William Wallace was led to the Tower, where he was stripped of his clothes, then dragged through the city at the heels of a horse. He was hanged, drawn and quartered – strangled by hanging, taken down while still alive, emasculated, eviscerated and his bowels burned before him, beheaded, then cut into four parts.

August 1st and 2nd: Jousting Tournament, 11.30 and 4.30pm

Not since the Tudor period has the Tower hosted a traditional jousting tournament. Henry VIII and his new Queen, Anne Boleyn, were to be seen in the moat, watching as the knights fought it out with each other (though thankfully not to the death, this time).

Chris Gidlow says:

We couldn't do it with solid lances (because of the ground surface), so we did it with balsa lances like you customarily see and made it look as realistic as possible. We got the armour worked up so it looked authentic to the Henry VIII era and used the Westminster tournament roll to work out what the stand would have looked like. So as far as the visitors could see, it was an entirely realistic tournament. We made sure that the characters jousting were known people and we talked about who they were and how they were connected to each other, like Sir Nicholas Carew was one of the Tower victims, as it turns out, so we did his story. Henry Grey, Jane Grey's father, was also one of the participants. That tournament was an absolute labour of love for me, so enjoyable to put together, and I look forward to many more.

Spectacular jousting tournament

August 2nd: A Yeoman Warder in His Castle

Happy birthday

Uniforms hanging

Outside his house

Yeoman Warder Shaun Huggins celebrates his birthday today. Shaun joined the Royal Anglian Regiment at age sixteen as a machine-gunner and at the same time joined their Corps of Drums as a boy drummer. He worked through the ranks to become Warrant Officer Class 1 (WO1), as well as the Senior Drum Major (Army), and left in 2011, having achieved twenty-six years' service and been stationed all around the world, to join the Tower as a probationer.

His wife Dawn and their teenage son Joshua joined him once he had finished his probationary six months and this family now lives in a four-storey house in the walls of the Tower, with a main room on each of the four floors. Privacy is of extra importance to them, not least (I guess) because of living on the job, in part of the Tower which still makes up 'the story' that is being presented to the public 362 days of the year, and yet needing to be able to separate work from leisure. I felt doubly privileged when Shaun said I would be welcome to visit his home. It felt so personal and warmly welcoming. Tasteful army memorabilia was on display and my breath was taken away when I stepped up to the first landing: displayed on the wall was a great picture of Shaun and his wife Dawn, who had achieved the same WO1 rank in the Adjutant General's Corps. It was a stunning example of just how enormous these people are – the years of successful devotion to duty, the authority, the dignity, the specialist skills et al. Within the Tower, this couple isn't necessarily exceptional, but similar to so many others, who have started on the bottom rung of the ladder and gradually climbed to the top, aspiring to excellence. I mentioned to Shaun that despite all the austere grey stonework, their home had a cosy, genteel atmosphere. He replied that Dawn sorted that out – she had the place in order within four weeks (I wouldn't doubt it)!

Shaun often does the Sunday chapel duty and I do enjoy his dramatic timing and rhythm when performing 'the story' (no wonder he made top drummer). According to the local newspaper, he captivated the children and staff when he addressed classes at a school in Bushey recently. Headteacher Claire Aisthorpe said:

Shaun the Beefeater was so charismatic and entertaining that we could have listened to him and asked him questions for hours and hours. The girls really enjoyed his visit and learned a lot.

August 16th: So What's Wrong? Me!

Sensing great agitation and tension on arrival to talk with one of the Yeoman Serjeants, I offered to disappear and come back another day, but was told that it was OK. What was wrong? Had someone tried to steal the Crown Jewels? Had there been a major fire? The phone rang and the message was obviously important news! The relief was enormous – joy and delight suddenly filled the room, and then I was given the explanation: the drains had been blocked and it had taken a very long time to clear. Apparently the stench in some parts of the Tower was virtually unbearable, even in the open air. Unfortunately, the problem is not easy to resolve; the sewers are antiquated and the numbers of people passing through far exceed the numbers they were designed for. Afterwards, there were lots of giggles and funny looks as I walked around, but I guess it must have been upsetting, because everyone just wants the best experience for the visitor – such is life!

A great stink

Interview with Yeoman Serjeant Bob Loughlin

After completing thirty-six years' service (that's twice the Long Service Medal length) Bob became Chief of the Air Staff's Warrant Officer, the senior Warrant Officer in the Royal Air Force. Based in Whitehall, he worked for three different chiefs of staff, including Sir Peter Squire GCB, DFC, AFC, DL, FRAeS, Sir Jock Stirrup KG, GCB, AFC, FRAeS, FCM and Sir Glenn Torpy GCB, CBE, DSO. Previously, Bob had done every job from parade grounds and drill to parachuting and administration, in various areas around the world.

In State dress, ready to be supervising with the Queen's birthday gun salute

Several friends were already at the Tower and it was still a progression following retirement. Within two years he was promoted to Serjeant and he is emphatic about still loving the work. In this picture, he is wearing his state dress, because it was the Queen's birthday and he was soon to be taking part in supervising the gun salute. His gentle smile and demeanour could confuse the unknowing; behind lies a huge wealth of knowledge, skills and leadership experience. You can listen to his voice on a very interesting recording on the University of Huddersfield website: http://www.hud.ac.uk/research/researchcentres/aaarg/projects/yeomanwarders/oral-history/

One of Serjeant Bob's responsibilities is overseeing 'the salvage team', which involves him with a group of colleagues, dealing with health and safety issues. An important document is written for each area, which gives specific details about action in the event of an emergency; this covers visitor and staff safety, fire drills and security issues, and lists which items should be rescued (where possible) in order of priority. An obvious, simplified example if a fire developed in the Fusilier Museum would be making fire-fighting arrangements while evacuating people, then saving Victoria Cross medals first if possible etc. This requires specialist knowledge, a great eye for detail, constant preparation, review, update and practice.

Bob's wife Diana worked at the White Tower until recently (having trained by learning the White Tower 'story') and their main home is in Suffolk. He likes to point out that 'an Englishman's home is his castle – in my case it's true!'

August 25th: Ghosts – Well, Why Not?

It was late evening as I passed the Byward Tower, close to the Main Gate, when I realised I had left my notebook behind in the Yeoman Warders' Bar, at the far end of Water Lane. On returning, yes, I was thinking about the eerie spookiness of the Tower at night. I looked to the right (towards the doctor's surgery and Old Mint) and there, peering through the window, was an illuminated white, shrouded figure. There is no doubt that it wasn't there previously when I passed.

I hadn't noticed before, but this gadget is permanently displayed in the window and projects various images. It can be switched on at times to suit, so I assume that someone had spotted an easy victim. OK, guys, it was a great scam and, yes, I nearly jumped out of my skin. Ho ho ho!

Anecdote:

An American tourist asked, 'How many dumb questions do you get asked in a day?'
I replied, 'Yours could be the first.'
He said, 'Good, I have lots more for you.'
Contributor: Yeoman Warder Kevin Kitcher

Clever joke at my expense

September 2015

September 2nd 1666: The Great Fire of London starts in Pudding Lane. For three days and three nights, the fire raged, destroying much of the old city. To protect the Tower, nearby buildings were pulled down, so no damage was done.

September 6th: Saint Peter ad Vincula Morning Service:
                 The Buffs Association

Today, the Buffs made their annual visit to the Chapel Royal. During the service, they presented a new hymn board, which was dedicated by the Rt Revd Nigel Stock, Bishop to HM Forces.

'Steady the Buffs' originates either from the Colonel slowing down his regiment's advance in the Peninsular War, or from the competitive spirit between the Buffs and Fusiliers garrisoned together in Malta. Whichever, Canon Roger was certainly inspired with steadiness when, on accepting the impressive gift during the service, he nimbly reached high up on the wall to take down the heavy old hymn board and then replaced it confidently with the smart new one!

Proud veterans on parade

September 14th: Yeoman Warder Moira Cameron

Another proud moment

Moira Cameron is currently the only female Yeoman Warder. Previously she served in the army with the Royal Army Pay Corps and saw service abroad in Northern Ireland and Cyprus. I understand that it's more difficult to recruit the ladies because there are far fewer in the services.

Moira has been particularly pleased to be mentoring probationer Spike Abbott. One of the reasons is that Spike replaced Yeoman Serjeant Crawford Butler when he retired and Crawford had been Moira's mentor. She mentions that Spike is similar to Crawford in some ways and she has a good friendship with him (as often evolves between mentor and probationer). Spike is former RAF and was an Air Load Master; he has a particular interest in the history of Lady Jane Grey.

Staff at the Jewel House and the White Tower also look extremely smart and polished. They gain a great wealth of knowledge and speak to individuals and groups with enthusiasm and vigour. Like the Yeoman Warders, they face a constant barrage of questions and become skilled in dealing with the day-to-day pressures of managing large numbers in confined places. Children often ask the ladies whether they are Moira Cameron (the well-known lady Yeoman Warder) and they explain, 'No, I am not a Beefeater.'

September 18th: Rugby World Cup Trophy

The Rugby World Cup trophy came close to the end of its hundred-day around-the-country tour at the Tower of London yesterday. The Webb Ellis Trophy (which is stunningly beautiful, incidentally) stayed with the Crown Jewels in the Jewel House overnight, before leaving the Tower on its final journey to Twickenham, carried by former England captain Lawrence Dallaglio, escorted by Yeoman Serjeant Jim Duncan and Yeoman Warder Clive Towel.

My Christian faith was severely tested when walking around the Tower this evening, relaxed and thinking beautiful thoughts. There, beamed onto the wall, was a huge picture of legendary All Blacks captain Richie McCaw – who (with numerous predecessors) had given my fellow Welshmen such a punishing time at Cardiff Arms Park and the new Millenium Stadium. However, we did learn to be 'good sports' as kids, so I am pleased to recommend this short video of their visit to the Tower: http://www.allblacks.com/Video/Viewer/24628/all-blacks-welcomed-at-the-tower-of-london

The William Webb Ellis Trophy

September 20th: A French Tour Guide's Perspective

While waiting to start one of her tours on Tower Wharf, Amandine Korrigan was pleased to express her views about her long-standing passion for the Tower. She said:

Young sentry trained not to make noise while marching close to Queen's House

> I was twenty-one when I came here first. I remember it as a dark, grey place, full of empty rooms, as if the people from the past had deserted it.
>
> I had no idea when studying England's history that I'd be back here for real.
>
> The Romans created Londinium and their ancient wall remains close to the Tower. The Normans used this protection and built the magnificent White Tower inside the fortification.
>
> The Tower of London still stands, representing power, protection, respect and the union of kingdoms, the perfect symbol of the grand city that is London.
>
> I always feel honoured and emotional to be here. The rooms don't seem empty anymore, because I now see William the Conqueror, Anne Boleyn, Josef Jakobs and so many others. I admire the traditions that continue, like the Ceremony of the Keys and the Queen's Guards not being allowed to make noise with their boots before the Queen's House. The Tower of London not only secures the Crown Jewels but the heritage of our civilisation.

September 24th: Sir Thomas More's Cell

I hadn't previously visited the Thomas More cell, so I was thrilled when Yeoman Serjeant Pete McGowran suggested that he could show me, particularly since he had often mentioned his own admiration for the man, who is regarded as a saint by the Catholic Church. Pete had been standing by the tomb while the Queen was signing the visitors' book during her recent visit, and also attended the occasion when Cardinal Nichols prayed with the Bishop of London in the cell.

Lady Dannatt had recently mentioned her experience that people often show emotion when viewing the cell, and I was feeling quite apprehensive on entering. There was certainly an immediate impact – my personal experience of the Tower, its religious significance and its history all came together here at this moment. Pete quietly explained where he had stood with choir members while Cardinal Nichols, the Bishop of London and Chaplain Roger joined together in honouring the memory of Sir Thomas. I deeply savoured the privilege, occasion and power of this unforgettable experience.

The following links are useful for further information and the videos give a good impression of the cell and its distinguished visitors.

Catholic Herald, 'Archbishop Nichols prays with Bishop of London in More's cell': http://www.catholicherald.co.uk/news/2013/10/24/archbishop-nichols-prays-with-bishop-of-london-in-mores-cell/

The Telegraph, 'A night in the shadow of Sir Thomas More': http://www.telegraph.co.uk/history/10390989/A-night-in-the-shadow-of-Sir-Thomas-More.html

When interviewing the Bishop of London, I asked his view about Sir Thomas More and he said:

I'm actually much more devoted to John Fisher, as is my friend the Cardinal [Cardinal Vincent Nichols, Catholic Archbishop of Westminster], who's a Fisher man really and has written about John Fisher.

September 24th: Portrait of Canon Roger

I have just heard that a portrait of Canon Roger is being painted. The artist is Gina Rule, a well-established portrait painter and friend of the Barkers, who attend services regularly. I am told that the painting is in oil on canvas and that she met Roger Hall for two sittings, the first being in June 2015. She then worked from the many photographs taken from their first meeting. Gina says:

I wanted to paint Roger before I actually met him. Why? It was the word of ordinary people who knew Roger and spoke to me about him with such warmth and joy, affection and respect. I heard of a sermon he had preached in which he spoke of someone he greatly admired who had kept their feet on the ground but their eyes firmly on Heaven. When Roger agreed to sit for me, this was the special quality I saw in him and this was the inspiration for my work.

Fitting portrait

Anecdote:

A lady asked me to explain what the wall was between the east side of the Bloody Tower and the Broadwalk Steps. I explained that it was part of the Great Hall of King Henry III.
'What happened to him?' she asked.
'He died,' I replied.
'Gee, I'm sorry. I heard about Princess Diana, but I didn't know the King had also died.'

Contributor: Yeoman Warder Tom Sharpe

October 2015

October 14th 1066: William the Conqueror wins the Battle of Hastings, defeating King Harold II and ending the Anglo-Saxon era.

October 4th: Saint Peter ad Vincula, Harvest Festival

Canon Roger Hall was extra delighted today – the congregation had dug deep to bring all kinds of produce and he was deeply appreciative. The gifts would be sent to the East London food bank, which is continually supported by the Chapel Royal. Roger and Cortland rightly remind us regularly that hunger and poverty in the East End is very close by and Roger's favourite slogan is 'buy two, get one free and bring it in on Sunday for the food bank'.

Gill Howard, a congregation member who is a volunteer with the Tower Hamlets food bank, says:

> *The Chapels Royal are key supporters, among several others in the area. The organisation is run by the First Love Foundation and unfortunately is much in need in the borough, which, despite housing the highly affluent Canary Wharf complex, has 49% of its children living below the poverty line. Over 250 organisations in Tower Hamlets have the ability to refer people they see and who are experiencing financial crisis to the food bank. It not only provides a week's worth of groceries to each client but also valuable welfare rights advice and support through the food bank's close working relationship with the Child Poverty Action Group.*

The music is always exceptional, for reasons explained elsewhere. Nevertheless, today was an extra treat with beautiful interpretations of two classics: Mozart's 'Te Deum' and 'The Heavens Are Telling the Glory of God' from Haydn's *Creation*.

Below left: *The church at work*

Below right: *Preparing for this colourful, symbolic service*

October 11th: Saint Peter ad Vincula Morning Service:
              Commemorating One Hundred Years Since
              Edith Cavell Was Executed

Our special guests today were the Ilford Paras Association; as always, the guest veterans were warmly welcomed. Canon Roger talked movingly about how Nurse Edith Cavell was executed in Belgium, one hundred years ago, on October 12th 1915. Having been trained at the Royal London Hospital, she is particularly famous for helping more than 200 Allied troops to escape German-occupied Belgium to safety in the Netherlands, and for saying, 'I realise that patriotism is not enough. I must have no hatred or bitterness towards anyone.'

The Dannatts have an association with Miss Cavell and the Constable comments:

She was the daughter of the vicar of St Mary's Swardeston, a little village in Norfolk. At one stage in her life as a young girl, she was governess to some members of my wife's family, so we're sort of quite close to Edith Cavell and her story, and she's buried in the grounds of Norwich Cathedral. In the past, I've been involved with the Cavell Nurses' Trust. So, in the context of Poppies and the nightly reading of the roll of honour, I thought we couldn't do it on the hundredth anniversary because the poppies would have gone, but to read her name on the ninety-ninth anniversary would be an appropriate thing to do. I was

Ilford Parachute Regimental Association

doing the reading that night and we added the name of Nurse Edith Cavell. To make it even more special, we also invited the choir from Norwich School to come and visit the Tower and then to sing in the moat, to perform after reading the roll of honour, which I think worked very well. We did hem and haw about amplifying the singing, but it would have cost up to £6,000, so I'm afraid we took the view that it would be money taken away from the Poppies, good causes and charities. Actually, the choir singing was perfect as it was. It wasn't that loud, but you could hear it if you were anywhere near and I thought it made a very special occasion. It also linked the Cavell story and the Cavell Nurses' Trust to the Tower of London, as well as Norwich, Norwich School, Norwich Cathedral and St Mary's Swardeston.

October 19th: The Tower Earning Its Keep!

One year ago today, members of the congregation joined other volunteers in the moat and achieved assembling and planting more than 1,000 poppies. 2015 is a comparatively quiet year for the Tower. Chief Yeoman Warder Alan says, 'The last three years for me have been the busiest three years in history because everything has been thrown at us. Now it's flat.'

In recent years, there has been involvement with royal celebrations, then the Olympics (incidentally, the medals were stored in the Jewel House and taken out daily). Then a rest? No! Following a phone call from Paul Cummins to the Tower, it became the focus for London, seemingly almost under siege, with cohorts of volunteers coming inside and millions of spectators passing by outside. Next year will see celebrations for the Queen's ninetieth birthday and the installation of the new Constable. And so the Tower continues to evolve in order to contribute, to stay central in importance and to raise enough money to pay for itself.

History and power

Complex renovation

The new steps

October 22nd: The New White Tower Steps Are Open From Today

Construction of the steps has taken fifty oak trees from South Oxfordshire, hand-hewn with an assortment of axes by traditional craftsmen. This short film made by HRP gives the full story: http://www.hrp.org.uk/conservation/conservation-projects/conservation-at-the-tower-of-london/the-white-tower-staircase-project/

October 23rd: Royal Armouries Exhibition: The Battle of Agincourt. Oct 23rd 2015 to Jan 31st 2016

The Royal Armouries is the United Kingdom's national museum of arms and armour, and one of the most important museums of its type in the world. The main exhibition was in the White Tower, with a very ambitious re-enactment involving the public in the moat.

Chris Gidlow says:

> *If you came [to the exhibition] it was solid and vibrant. We had people re-enacting the prisoners of the Tower of London, the soldiers from the battlefield, the public going down and fighting out the battle ... there was everything you could have wanted from the interpretation.*

October 24: Quiet Day, Royal Foundation of St Katharine's, Limehouse

The Reverend Cortland Fransella led the proceedings, which included Holy Communion in the chapel, a pleasant lunch, lively discussion and an opportunity to reflect and get to know each other better.

It was especially poignant for me, having already written a book about St Katharine's (*The Story of St Katharine's*, Cloister

Royal foundation of St Katharine, Lime House

House, 2014). Links abound between the Tower and its next-door neighbour, the original hospital and precinct of St Katharine's (from 1148). For example, the east part of the moat originally belonged to St Katharine's – it had been a mill, other buildings and a garden, and was sold to the Tower around 1190 so that the Tower could complete its moat.

In the north-west corner of the chapel is the Holland memorial, which was moved here in 1951 from the chapel of the Royal Hospital of St Katharine at Regent's Park (removed from the original hospital in 1825, before it was demolished to make way for the Telford Docks). John Holland was a direct descendant of Edward I and was created Duke of Exeter in 1444 while Constable of the Tower. He and his family were important bene-factors of St Katharine's and it is known that nearby citizens, maybe involved in defending the Tower, practised their crossbow skills using shooting ranges on its neighbour's land. Holland was present when a man was accidentally killed as a bolt glanced off a tree. The Duke expressly willed to be buried in a tomb chantry on the north side of the High Altar, with his first wife, his sister and his wife of the time. Today's chapel at Limehouse holds numerous relics from the original hospital, including the pulpit in which Canon Roger's predecessor preached the final sermon at St Katharine's.

It is likely that Henry VIII was fond of St Katharine's – he had built the Queen's House for Anne Boleyn during their courting period and often visited the Tower. He appointed four of his queens to be patron and he didn't abuse the hospital during his national purge of religious organisations.

Bishop Richard says, 'I'm glad to think of it [the Chapel Royal] serving the St Katharine's community again, which is one of the features of the life of St Peter ad Vincula.'

October 25th: Saint Peter's ad Vincula Morning Service

The special guests today are the City of London Royal Marine Reserves. This division was created in 1948 at a ceremonial parade on Bunhill Fields (just north of the City of London), where, significantly, the Corps of Royal Marines was originally formed in October 1664.

October 27th: Twilight Tour: Yeoman Clerk Phil Wilson

Yeoman Clerk Phillip is considered an authority on the many ghost and ghoul stories at the Tower and is expert (among experts) at delivering a good tale. On this occasion, he took a party of 300 around in the dark and I was told that a good number of them left very quietly afterwards and didn't sleep well. HRP have posted a short video about him and ghost stories on YouTube: https://www.youtube.com/watch?v=ukj5vpRJjPM

Phil Wilson's rank is one above the Serjeants and he loves deputising for Gaoler. This is some of what he has to say:

The great story teller

> *On leaving school, I went straight into the army. I'm now reaching sixty-five this year and I've never had a day of unemployment. I left school on Friday and went to the army, left the army on Friday and started work here on Monday, never had a break. I did my first guard here in 1968 as a young guardsman and I still think I'm the only Yeoman Warder that has done the Ceremony of the Keys from every aspect except the Officer of the Guard. I've been the Serjeant of the Guard, the Corporal of the Guard, done the Challenge, carried the lantern, been the watchman, and of course I've been the duty supervisor and locked the Tower.*
>
> *My work involves dealing with security clearance for the Ceremony of the Keys and for contractors, plus I also do all the tailoring, uniform ordering, the hat ordering, that sort of thing. My background was also master tailor in the Coldstream Guards.*
>
> *I always enjoy doing the guided tour, but you've got to deliver it like it's the first time you've ever done it because it's the first time that the audience has ever heard it, and on top of that they're on holiday. They want to know the facts, but they also want to be entertained.*
>
> *The Yeoman body is changing, it's got to, it always has evolved. If you look at the White Tower or the Jewel House, the staff there change far more than they used to. When I came*

here, the Tower had only just started to be Historic Royal Palaces; before that it was run by the government's Department of Works – there was no such thing as a budget, it was just a big pocket of government expenditure and that's how everything went. When it changed to HRP there were budgets and we had to make money. I think that makes people move on, it just becomes part of the circle of life, whereas when it was government, it was your whole life. People would start here on a civil service pension and stay until they drew it.

Upkeep is expensive but necessary. I've been here for nineteen years and I think there was only a period of five months when there was no scaffolding at the Tower. But then again it's now still standing. If it weren't for that scaffolding, it wouldn't be. It's a living thing. I can remember going to America and I went to the White House in Washington; it had scaffolding right up to the roof and I vowed that the first American who complained to me about scaffolding around the Tower was going to get it. Believe it or not, not one ever has!

My wife and I are so fortunate. We've had lunch at the White House, afternoon tea at Buckingham Palace, dinner with Cliff Richard and we live here at the Tower in historic accommodation, between the Tower's doctor and its chaplain, overlooking Tower Green. As I got the job here I said to my wife, 'I'm going to take you to live in a Royal Palace.' Know what her answer was? 'Don't push it; it was a state prison!' You just don't realise you're part of English history. I do love it. You understand that if you really like what you do you're never going to work again in your life!

Scaffolding (disguised) at the Tower

The Ceremony of the Keys

The Ceremony of the Keys has taken place each night, without exception, for more than 700 years. Only once was it delayed slightly, when a bomb hit nearby during the Second World War. The purpose is to lock up the inner fortress, previously to protect the monarch and now, still, to protect the Crown Jewels and other priceless valuables. The short, elaborate ceremony involves the Queen's keys being marched from the main gate, being challenged by the guard; the Last Post is sounded and the inner gate is locked. Fifty visitors are allowed and I have observed it numerous times. Complete silence is expected and, like me, others are always deeply engaged and moved.

Anecdote:

A young girl from the USA, talking to me after a special: 'Did you really guard Rudolf Hess?'
'Yes, for two years, while stationed in Berlin.'
Shocked, she replies, 'But you don't look old enough to be around in 1941.' This fifty-five-year-old laughed a lot!

Contributor: Yeoman Warder Dave Phillips

November 2015

November 6th 1914: German Carl Hans Lody becomes the first spy to be executed at the Tower. He was the Tower's first prisoner in almost 100 years and its first execution in nearly 200 years. From his death until 11 April 1916, eleven men of various nationalities were held, tried and executed by firing squad for espionage.

November 1st: All Saints' Day, 'Celebrating the Saints'

The usual morning services took place, with an additional event in the afternoon to celebrate All Saints' Day at All Hallows by the Tower. There was a series of readings and music, preceded by a most enjoyable lunch at the adjacent restaurant 'The Kitchen'. It was intriguing to listen to Colm and the choir performing in this bigger and more splendid church; All Hallows has its famous wealth of history and is the oldest church in the City of London. This recently started tradition was appreciated and enjoyed by everyone.

Choir singing at nearby All Hallows by the Tower

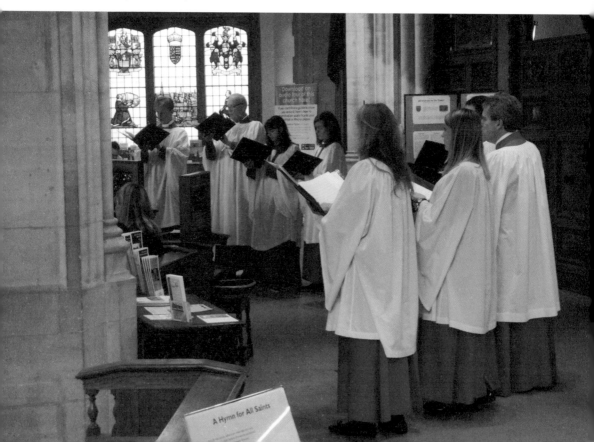

November 3rd: Evening Concert at St Peter ad Vincula:
                        The Raptured Soul

In the words of the organiser of this concert, 'Handel arias rubbed shoulders with jazz improvisations based on some of Handel's most well-known tunes.' Featuring Eleanor Harries, mezzo-soprano, who also sings regularly with the Chapels Royal choir. It was a varied and exciting musical evening within the setting of the beautiful Tudor Chapel Royal. Eleanor also organised this evening's concert and rightly seemed very pleased with the outcome. As Colm points out, the talent and expertise is here, ready to be further developed as another aspect of HRP and its success (see November 10th).

November 6th: Poppies at the Tower Again

Yeoman Gaoler Chris and his Yeoman Warder colleagues parade here every year during the Poppy Appeal. Each morning from 7.30 to 9.30, they can be seen engaging with the public, collecting for the Poppy Appeal. These high-ranking ex-services people never seem to stop – brilliant! Chris hopes to exceed £5,000 this year.

Selling poppies near Tower Hill underground station

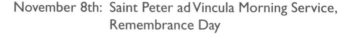

Highly symbolic soil from Flanders

November 8th: Saint Peter ad Vincula Morning Service, Remembrance Day

Quite a spectacle

During the service, Canon Hall read out several pieces of First World War poetry, and in the sermon he referred to his own experiences as an army chaplain, when death was always potentially close. While serving in Northern Ireland, he oversaw burying the dead every week, and in Armagh two soldiers had actually died in his arms. The regiment garrisoned for guard duty provided the bugle which played the Last Post.

The Salamander Relic was presented to Canon Roger Hall MBE, who placed it in its present location. Highly symbolic, the soil in this box was dug up from Passchendaele, leaving a hole that was filled in by soil from Galilee. On the box are lines from the First World War poem 'Into the Fire'. The box is made of wood from a barn in Ypres that had been shelled, and the relic was brought from Belgium by three members of the Yeoman Body.

November 10th: Evening Concert at St Peter ad Vincula: The Plague Maiden

The singers and instrumentalists of Ensemble Utopia presented a musical commemoration of Europe's struggle to overcome the bubonic plague. The programme included Matthias Weckmann's extraordinary cantata 'Wie liegt die Stadt so wüste', written after Hamburg suffered a devastating epidemic in 1663. It also featured works by several composers who died of the plague, together with uplifting music by Monteverdi to celebrate Venice's recovery from the plague in 1631. This was the second of two concerts featuring organiser Eleanor Harries (see November 3rd).

Eleanor and friends are excellent performers. These events were well appreciated and enjoyed by the audiences. There is also an exceptional mystique about the Tower when it is closed to the public in the evening, with the cobbles on Water Lane, the dominance of the ancient White Tower and looking across at Tower Bridge, all to be enjoyed by visitors attending the evening concerts – a great asset for this unique venue.

Interview with Cate Milton, Operations Programme Coordinator

There is a Tower diary, which is the main part of my job – making sure that everything that needs to happen at the Tower can occur, resolving potential clashes or conflicts over the space needed and keeping a record of what happens. I also organise some of the ceremonies such as the Ceremony of the Lilies and Roses and Constable's Dues. I am so lucky; ever since I was small, I've been passionate about the Tower of London. It was rather strange because I was here as a visitor just before Christmas 2013 and was on a Yeoman Warder tour with the Ravenmaster. He made a joke about being on Twitter because he looks after birds, so I got my phone out and followed him straight away. After that, it suggested that I might want to follow 'HRP_palaces' as well, so I did, and honestly, about two weeks later they tweeted about what became my absolute dream job. I simply adore the Tower. I love HRP, but this is my particular home.

The Tower has a life of its own

We've got so many stakeholders, it's not just HRP. We've got the Royal Armouries, Chapels Royal, the Royal Regiment of Fusiliers as well. The Tower is such a community and everybody has opportunities to have a say and I think that's so important and why it's so successful. I believe that it's the culture of HRP; it knows how important all the composite parts are in making a success.

I think it's an exciting time for the Tower because there's all sorts of work going on, research work where we're finding out all these additional stories and setting out the difference between the mythology of the place and the reality. It's not been given the Victorian Gothic treatment. Because we are such an infamous, famous site, every single year of those 900 years would have a phenomenal or remarkable story to tell, that affected not just the community here, but London, the rest of England, the rest of the Empire, the whole world. So it's such an important site.

The Tower has a life of its own now that is very different to what it was in the last 900 years, but it's just as relevant and important today. It's nice that people understand what we're trying to do and how much we care desperately about these buildings. We just want to look after them and keep them for another 900 years.

A day to remember

Fine new headquarters for the world famous Ravens

November 17th: Yeoman Serjeant James Duncan Is Decorated with the Royal Victoria Medal

Jim went to Buckingham Palace with his wife Eve today, to receive his medal from the Duke of Cambridge.

He was awarded the Royal Victoria Medal (Silver) in the Queen's Birthday Honours 2015. This was for his key role in supervising the *Blood Swept Lands and Seas of Red* installation at the Tower of London in 2014, commemorating the First World War centenary. 888,246 ceramic poppies were planted in the dry moat at the Tower, to complete a sculpture representing every British and colonial fatality of the First World War. The installation was a huge success and an estimated 5 million people came to see it. The poppies were sold individually, which raised millions of pounds for six service charities. More information can be found in Part Two.

November 18th: The Ravens Have Fine New Accommodation

The ravens are reported to be settling into their new, modern enclosure. They are expertly looked after by the Ravenmaster and his team. There is more information at http://www.hrp.org.uk/tower-of-london/visit-us/ top-things-to-see-and-do/the-ravens/

November 26th: Interview with Patrick Baty

HRP have often relied on Patrick Baty's experience as an acknowledged expert on the paint and colours of the past four centuries, creating schemes sympathetic to the aims of a particular space and its current and future use. He describes his analysis as a small and highly specialised field, requiring the combined skills of historian, detective and analyst. On this occasion, Patrick explained his recent work before this year's Queen's House renovation (see February 9th).

In September 2014 I was asked to examine the paint on the exterior of the Queen's House. The two-fold aim was to learn of its decorative history and also to provide information on the age of the different elements.

Samples were taken from representative doors, windows and other painted surfaces. These showed that two major refurbishments in the twentieth century had led to much loss of earlier paint. In spite of this, it was possible to form a reasonable idea of the treatment of the windows since the late seventeenth century and the door architraves from a century later.

I found a total of forty-nine schemes on one of the small sash windows and it seems highly likely that the first of these was applied in the 1680s. A sequence of off-whites can be seen until the beginning of the nineteenth century, when black was used. For the next hundred years, dark colours were employed, with another black followed by dark brown and then a deep dull red. Throughout the twentieth century off-whites and pale yellowish colours were adopted.

The doors and architraves had mostly been stripped, although paint evidence dating from the 1770s was found on one of the architraves. The vast majority of decorative schemes were considered to have been in variants of off-white or stone colour.

No information earlier than about 1914 was found on the doors themselves. They had either been stripped or replaced at various points. However, I could see that dark green had been used in the early twentieth century before the adoption of black. It seems that those doors that are now painted mid-blue were painted dark blue in the 1950s. The existing colour dates

What 49 layers of paint look like

Queen's House, renovation

from the late 1970s and almost certainly relates to the decorative scheme applied to Tower Bridge for the Queen's Silver Jubilee in 1977. There are some areas on Tower Green where both the bridge and the doors of the Queen's House can be seen at the same time. This probably led to them having a shared colour.

In spite of major work involving the removal of an external staircase tower and extensive window replacement in about 1914, tiny traces of earlier paint survived. The stripping of the original render in the 1960s also made things difficult for me. However, by taking a sufficient number of samples from carefully selected locations I was able to put together enough information to build a reasonable account of the changes that had taken place, regarding both structure and colour.

November 29th: Saint Peter ad Vincula Morning Service: Advent Carol Service

Great beginning to the Christmas season, though an extra busy time for Canon Roger Hall. This year, twenty-one carol services are booked.

Advent candles

Anecdote:

A French visitor looks at Queen's House from Tower Green – he starts to point out each house as Number 7, Number 8, Number 9, and then turns to me and asks, 'Is zee big one Number 10 Downing Street?'

'It's Christmas; just pour me a gin and tonic!'

Contributor: Yeoman Warder Ray Stones

December 2015

December 10th 1541: Thomas Culpeper and Francis Dereham were executed. Allegedly, both these men had affairs with Catherine Howard, Henry VIII's fifth wife.

5th December: A Relaxing Moment for Steve; How Demanding Is the Work?

Yeoman Warder Steve Froggatt was previously in the Royal Marines – here he is seen looking thoughtfully at the water during a short break. He works part-time in the Thames River Police and says that water is still a great passion for him.

I can only guess and speculate about the internal pressure of being a Yeoman Warder. As a Royal Marine, Steve would have learned more than most about coping strategies, about dealing with pressure and about survival. Later in life, these highly trained, experienced and successful individuals retrain, knowing that at the end of six months, they will need to impress upon first Yeoman Gaoler and then Chief Yeoman Warder that they have enough knowledge and can hold the attention of visitors well enough for forty-five minutes, three times a day. That's that, then – oh, no, it's not! As well as learning to field countless questions, they'll pose for photographs seemingly hundreds of times a day. Nor can it be easy learning to work closely with thirty-six other powerful characters. Out in all weather, they walk many miles each day. Most visitors are polite, but I have observed rudeness from children (both parents and teachers looking on, without correcting the child) and adults. I haven't discussed this with the Yeoman Warders, assuming they'd tell me that it's all roses (and lilies, of course). While I understand that the remuneration is quite good and the prestige and cheaper accommodation are big bonuses, my guess is that they earn every penny of the Queen's shilling.

Time for a moment's reflection and relaxation

December 6th: Anniversary of the Two Ronnies'
                'Yeomen of the Guard' Musical Sketch.

Earlier in the year, I was talking with two Yeoman Warders about their image in British culture. As we were chatting, they fondly recalled this sketch. Though dated, they rightly pointed out that it still sparkles with the same wit and liveliness that today's Yeoman Warders aspire to when telling the countless stories about the Tower. Thanks, guys, for persuading me on this one. I couldn't get any more information about who arranged it at the Tower, but it was broadcast by the BBC on 6th December 1980.

December 9th: Interview with
                Commander John Herriman DL RNR

John was appointed Executive Officer at HMS *President* in 2013, while remaining in post as the head of the RNR Diving Branch. He was promoted to Commander on 1 April 2014 and assumed command of HMS *President*. This is a part-time Reservist appointment and professionally he works as the Executive Director for an education trade union, alongside an academic lecturing career. As well as being a diving and bomb disposal expert, he holds a private pilot's licence and enjoys martial arts and spending time with his family.

Commander HMS President

Marching for HMS President's Annual Parade

HMS President has always had an association with the Tower but this became an even tighter bond when we moved to our current location in St Katharine Docks in 1988. We are privileged to be able to use it for our annual carol service and our annual Divisions in May [see May 26th]. This has been fabulous for the unit: to be allowed to march into the Tower and use it to parade as a Royal Naval Reserve unit in London. You can tell by the smile on my face, it's just one of those great things, marvellous!

Last night we had our annual carol service in the Chapel Royal of St Peter ad Vincula and it was packed. Vice Admiral the Rt Hon. the Lord Sterling of Plaistow GCVO CBE was a special guest because he is an honorary RNR officer, plus there were various other distinguished guests from our affiliated livery companies and the City, our ship's company and their families. The service was excellent, then it was back to HMS President for a hugely enjoyable Christmas dinner. Every few years we hold the carol service in a different church in the borough so we can reach out to the local community and this is always rewarding, but it is also great to return to the Tower because of everything it represents to us. The Tower of London definitely has an extra draw for families and friends, who always get excited at the prospect of having such privileged access for an incredibly special event. It is a great privilege for all of us. Long may it continue.

State gold on display

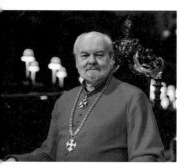

Bishop of London and Dean of the Royal Chapels

December 20th: Saint Peter ad Vincula Morning Service, State Parade and Service of Nine Carols and Lessons

There was an excellent atmosphere for this high point in the Christmas calendar, with all the colour, splendour and excitement that is associated with the occasion. Of note was that the chapel was filled to capacity and a number of people had to be turned away, which was, of course, quite upsetting.

December 21st: Interview with Rt Rev. and Rt Hon. Dr Richard Chartres, Bishop of London

I was surprised that Bishop Richard had allowed this time at such a peak period, but when I mentioned that I would be brief, he smiled calmly and said there were plenty of people to help out. Most striking was his expressed sense of involvement.

I always enjoy going to the Tower and of course, it is very anomalous – it being a Royal Palace, I'm there not as the Bishop of London but as Dean of Her Majesty's Chapels Royal.

Well, I think it's very remarkable, the efforts that have been made to secure the future of the chapel, because as you know it doesn't have a significant endowment, but it has some very dedicated supporters – an enormous amount of work has been done. I really love going every Maundy Thursday, just before Easter. I think it's a tradition which I've established and I've done it now for twenty years.

Clearly, museums have changed in our lifetime – they're no longer repositories of dead objects, but places of fruitful and creative remembering, and places of ideas. I think it adds immeasurably to the attractions of the Tower that it isn't a dead museum, but a living community, including the ravens, certainly including the congregation of St Peter ad Vincula, and I'm glad to think of it serving the St Katharine's community again, which is one of the features of the life of St Peter ad Vincula, another way in which it is a very speaking place. There is a continuity of worship there. Every time we celebrate the Holy Eucharist, of course, we are doing something which unites us with the Church not only in every place but also in every time ... this was an enactment that was present when the White Tower was consecrated and dedicated in Norman times. Now one of the best things about Maundy Thursday is the presence of that learned and loyal person, Bernard, who never ceases to remind me about his own seriousness and commitment to the importance of what we are enacting. It is always a privilege to stand at the altar with him.

I was so delighted to witness one of the re-enactments that happen from time to time in the Tower. It was the escape of Bishop Flambard, who was the first person, I think, to be incarcerated in the Tower of London – he escaped dressed as a washerwoman or similar. Re-enactments are very much the stock-in-trade of Historic Royal Palaces. I have myself been mistaken for Cardinal Wolsey at Hampton Court, which I don't think was very polite, but there we are.

December 25th: Christmas Day. St Peter ad Vincula Morning Service

For this special day there was a short, pleasant, less formal Matins service. It was rare to see the Tower so quiet and peaceful at this time.

The 150 or so residents will hopefully make the most of the peace and quiet while the Tower is closed to the public. When empty of visitors, the Tower has a uniquely eerie, majestic and mystic aura.

Our favourite time for the Tower is when it's empty, just along the wharf or around the Tower, because it's very pleasant, you know, it's fabulous.

Pauline Dodd, Yeoman Warder's wife

Majestic, awesome, iconic

Enough, just for a few days

Water Lane 'at rest'

Walking around quietly afterwards, aware that this is the end of a year in the life of the Tower, I sensed the tiredness and the need for the Tower to take its well-deserved break. It was as if the whole place was crying out, 'Enough, just for a few days, we must rest.' All the carol services recently, the evening events, the tours every half-hour right through the year, the schoolchildren every day, the crowds climbing the steps to the White Tower and the constant streaming through the Jewel House. How many times had I been in myself, while observing for the book? And yet I hadn't witnessed a time when it was quiet and only small numbers of people were joining the tour. Close to 3 million visitors came through the gates during 2015. The Tower is so popular because it is packed full of personalities, history, humour, pressure, pride, tradition and, in particular, the telling of stories.

December 31st: Auld Lang Syne

Where the Tower community gather to sing Auld Lang Syne on New Year's Eve

Traditionally, most of us gather together towards midnight and sing this song with family and friends. Living nearby, I usually take champagne up onto Tower Bridge and look across, past the Tower below and London Bridge, along the Thames towards Westminster, and wait for midnight and the annual fireworks display. Down on Tower Wharf (hours since closed to the public), the residents, families and friends gather similarly, ready to toast in the New Year. As the song says, it's about time gone by, remembering family, friends and others from the past and not letting them be forgotten. This unique group celebrates similarly, but the residents are also careful to remember the Tower of London's past, all the historical figures and their own part in its current history.

Quip:

It's nice to know that even Bill Gates, with all of his billions, can't have my address.

Yeoman Warder Moira Cameron

A Final Word

"It does astonish me how many people don't believe there are residents in the Tower. This became very apparent to me when my wife and I did a bit of shopping and took a taxi back from Oxford Street. I told the driver we wanted to go to the Tower."

'Tower Bridge?'

'No, Tower of London, please.'

'It's closed.'

I said, 'Yes, I know, I live there.'

He said, 'No, you don't.'

I said, 'Yes, I do.'

'OK,' he said.

Eventually, we arrived and he said, 'Here's the Tower of London.'

I said, 'I know, keep going, through the gates.'

He said, 'You can't go through there.'

I said, 'Go down through the gates,' which he did.

At the gate, I said to the Yeoman Warder on duty, 'Hello, Kevin. You all right?'

He said, 'Yeah, right, fine, Phil.'

I directed the driver all the way around until we reached the other side by the chapel where the ancient tower is. I said, 'Do you see the top of that tower?'

'Yes.'

'That's where I live.' And then I said, 'How much is that?' and he said, 'I can't charge you.'

'Really?'

'No, you taught me a good lesson!'

Yeoman Clerk Phil Wilson
Beauchamp Tower

Part Two
Poppies
A phenomenon brilliantly achieved

Sketch by Jane Young

The 'Poppies' event in 2014 was to mark one hundred years since the first full day that Britain was involved in the First World War. Poppies grow naturally in the wild following large-scale disturbance of soil, so grew abundantly following the mass shelling that took place in the battlefields of World War I, creating beauty from destruction.

The British Legion was formed in 1921 and adopted the poppy as its symbol, manufacturing artificial poppies to sell and raise money for veterans and their families in its annual Poppy Appeal. For many years it has been a proud British tradition to wear a poppy in the days preceding Remembrance Day, November 11th, to remember members of the British armed forces who were killed, and those who fought alongside them.

Key players:

Paul Cummins: The artist who came up with the original idea for the poppies.

Tom Piper: Poppies Set Director. Directed the setting of poppies in the moat.

Col. John Brown, Deputy Governor, Tower of London: Initiated discussions before becoming Site Director for the sculpture.

Deborah Shaw, Head of Creative Programming and Interpretation, Historic Royal Palaces: Brought the initial concept into production and initiated the early project management.

Yeoman Warder Jim Duncan: Production Supervisor throughout.

Julian Cree: Earlier stage Production Manager.

Major Kirsty Baxter: Later stage Production Manager.

Lord Dannatt, Constable of the Tower of London: Offered constant advice and support; liaised with charities.

How 'Poppies' succeeded is complex and involved. These experienced, key people were each able to contribute their expert skills, inspiring first each other and then the numbers of people that would be needed to ensure success. How it was achieved in such a short space of time is a tribute to the dedication of these players and key organisation leaders, and to the warm-hearted generosity of the legions of volunteers. All of which led to a fitting memorial for the 888,246 heroes represented by the Poppies sculpture.

It could not have happened without this incredible collaboration between art, logistics and military; it was a perfect combination.

Deborah Shaw

Sea of red

On top of his work as Deputy Governor, Col. Brown steered the early discussions and planning meetings, setting up a charity status company to regularise the finances. He directed the project to its conclusion and was awarded an MBE for his leadership role.

It was a huge project and in effect, there was only a nine-month run-up, so we were totally focused on what we needed to achieve and half the problem I had leading that project was stopping others from being distracted. This was quite tough because if we'd had three years to plan, we could see that there were so many other things that could be done, but no, we didn't have the horsepower or the time, so we had to just crack on! Yes, it far exceeded our expectations and it has been a huge collaboration.

Col. John Brown

The collaboration began with the brilliantly inspired idea of Paul Cummins, an accomplished ceramic artist.

Paul Cummins

Paul was born in Chesterfield. His early career was in architectural design, later studying for his BA (Hons) degree at Derby University, where he further developed his knowledge and skills

Ceramic poppy

Photograph: Shirley Bailey

in ceramics and craft, passing in 2010. Paul developed his own studio, from where he could manufacture his ceramics, and worked on prestigious projects including large-scale installations for Chatsworth House, Derby Royal Hospital, Althorp Estate, Blenheim Palace, the Conran Shop, and other high-profile displays.

His idea for the Tower installation was inspired by the will of an unnamed soldier, which he found while searching old records in his hometown of Chesterfield; it included a poem, which began, 'The blood swept lands and seas of red'. This inspired him to create a large-scale installation, a sea of handmade ceramic poppies mounted on metal stems, to be placed in the moat around the Tower of London. Each poppy would represent the life of a person who died during the First World War; from research, he found that there would need to be 888,246, the total number of British and Colonial lives lost. His vision was for this sculpture to become a lasting and meaningful experience for the public; could he have had any idea just how important it was to become and the numbers of people it would touch and inspire?

One can only imagine the feelings and strain as the artist pushed forward with his idea. He approached the Tower of London – his luck held because it was not usual to reach 'senior management' straight away, but when Paul phoned, the Deputy Governor, Col. John Brown, agreed to speak to him, mistakenly thinking it was another person he knew with the same name. Various discussions took place where Paul pitched the idea and showed concept drawings of the project, and others joined the team.

Mr Cummins and his colleagues set about producing the ceramic poppies at his factory in Derby. The task was enormous, despite having eleven months before the deadline, so two other ceramics factories were commissioned to take much of the pressure, though Paul Cummins personally oversaw the retraining of everyone involved. Unfortunately, he suffered a serious personal injury, losing one of his fingers during production, but nevertheless his vision was fulfilled, a dream come true.

The final installation has been described as 'a world phenomenon' and has touched the hearts of so many people internationally, as well as in this country. Mr Cummins has received various honours and been personally honoured by the Queen. She was seen to have been deeply moved when she and the Duke of Edinburgh walked amongst the poppies.

Mr Cummings has recently been studying for a PhD, again at Derby, and is currently involved extensively in new projects. He is